ROYAL COURT

D0231311

Royal Court Theatre presents

MOUTH TO MOUTH

by **Kevin Elyot**

First performance at the Royal Court Jerwood Theatre Downstairs,
Sloane Square, London on 1 February 2001.

MOUTH TO MOUTH

by **Kevin Elyot**

Cast in order of appearance
Frank **Michael Maloney**
Laura **Lindsay Duncan**
Gompertz **Adam Godley**
Dennis **Peter Wight**
Phillip **Andrew McKay**
Cornelia **Lucy Whybrow**
Roger **Barnaby Kay**

Director **Ian Rickson**
Designer **Mark Thompson**
Lighting Designer **Hugh Vanstone**
Sound Designer **Paul Arditti**
Composer **Stephen Warbeck**
Choreographer **Quinny Sacks**
Musician **Sabbo**
Assistant Director **Nina Raine**
Assistant Designer **James Humphrey**
Assistant Lighting Designer **David Holmes**
Casting Director **Lisa Makin**
Production Manager **Paul Handley**
Company Stage Manager **Cath Binks**
Stage Management **Marion Marrs, Sara Crosdale, Linda Mary Wise**
Costume Supervisor **Iona Kenrick**
Company Voice Work **Patsy Rodenburg**

Royal Court Theatre would like to thank the following for their help with this production:
Jack Summerside, Gordon Strang, Maurice Grosse, Shamil Wanigaratne, Wardrobe care by Persil and
Comfort

THE COMPANY

Kevin Elyot (writer)
For the Royal Court: My Night With Reg.
Other theatre includes: Coming Clean (Bush);
Artists and Admirers (new translation, RSC); The
Day I Stood Still (RNT).
Screenplays include: Killing Time, The Moonstone
(adaptation), My Night With Reg.
Awards include the Samuel Beckett Award for
Coming Clean and a Writers' Guild award for his
screenplay Killing Time. For My Night With Reg,
Kevin received the Evening Standard, Laurence
Olivier, Writers' Guild and London Theatre
Critics' Circle awards.

Paul Arditti (sound designer)
Paul Arditti has been designing sound for theatre
since 1983. He currently combines his post as
Head of Sound at the Royal Court (where he has
designed more than 60 productions) with regular
freelance projects.
For the Royal Court: Spinning Into Butter, I Just
Stopped By to See The Man, Far Away, My Zinc
Bed, 4.48 Psychosis, Fireface, Mr Kolpert, The
Force of Change, Hard Fruit, Other People, Dublin
Carol, Breath, Boom, The Glory of Living, The
Kitchen, Rat in the Skull, Some Voices, Mojo, The
Lights, The Weir; The Steward of Christendom,
Shopping and Fucking, Blue Heart (co-productions
with Out of Joint); The Chairs (co-production with
Theatre de Complicite); The Strip, Never Land
(co-production with The Foundry), Cleansed, Via
Dolorosa, Real Classy Affair, My Night With Reg (&
West End).
Other theatre includes: Light (Complicite); Our
Lady of Sligo (RNT with Out of Joint); Some
Explicit Polaroids (Out of Joint); Hamlet, The
Tempest (RSC); Orpheus Descending, Cyrano de
Bergerac, St Joan (West End); Marathon (Gate).
Musicals includes: Doctor Dolittle, Piaf, The
Threepenny Opera.
Awards include: Drama Desk Award for
Outstanding Sound Design 1992 for Four Baboons
Adoring the Sun (Broadway).

Lindsay Duncan
For the Royal Court: Ashes to Ashes, Top
Girls (transferred to Jo Papp's Public Theater
in New York).
Other theatre includes: Celebration, The
Room (Almeida); Ashes to Ashes (Gramercy,
New York); The Homecoming, Berenice, Cat
on a Hot Tin Roof, Plenty, The Provok'd Wife,
The Prince of Homburg (RNT); A
Midsummer's Night Dream (RSC Barbican/
The Lunt Fontanne, New York) The Merry
Wives of Windsor, Troilus & Cressida (RSC
Stratford & Barbican); Les Liaisons
Dangereuses (RSC Stratford & Barbican/
Ambassadors/Music Box Theatre, New York);
The Cryptogram (Ambassadors); Three
Hotels (Tricycle); The Rivals, Zack, Twelfth
Night, What The Butler Saw, The Skin of Our
Teeth, The Ordeal of Gilbert Pinfold (Royal
Exchange, Manchester); Don Juan, Comings
and Goings, Incident at Tulse Hill, Hedda
Gabler (Hampstead); Progress (Bush); Julius
Caesar (Riverside Studios); Recruiting Officer
(Bristol Old Vic/ Edinburgh Festival).
Television includes: Family Tree, Dirty Tricks,
Oliver Twist, Shooting the Past, Tom Jones,
Get Real, Jake's Progress, The Rector's Wife,
A Year in Provence, Redemption, The
Childeater, Traffik, G.B.H., Grown Ups, On
Approval, Rainy Day Women, Muck and Brass,
Kit Curran Show, Reilly Ace of Spies, The
Greek Myths.
Films include: Mansfield Park, An Ideal
Husband, A Midsummer's Night Dream, City
Hall, The Reflecting Skin, Prick Up Your Ears,
Loose Connections, Samson and Delilah, For
a Night of Love, Body Parts.
Awards include a New York OBIE for Top
Girls, the Evening Standard Best Actress
Award for Cat On A Hot Tin Roof, an F.I.P.A.
D'or for Traffik, a Drama Desk nomination for
Ashes to Ashes, a BAFTA Best Actress
nomination for G.B.H. and most recently a
BAFTA nomination for Shooting the Past. For
Liaisons Dangereuses Lindsay won an Olivier
Award for Best Actress and was also
nominated for a Tony.

Adam Godley
For the Royal Court: Mr Kolpert.
Other theatre includes: The Importance of Being Earnest (Theatre Royal Haymarket); Cleo, Camping, Emmanuelle and Dick (RNT/Olivier Award nomination for Best Supporting Actor); The Critic (Royal Exchange, Manchester); The Front Page, Cabaret (Donmar); The Wood Demon (Playhouse); Three Hours After the Marriage, The White Devil, The General From America (RSC); A Midsummer Night's Dream (RSC/CLS concert); A Going Concern (Hampstead); The Rivals (Chichester Festival Theatre/Albery); The Revengers Comedies (Strand); June Moon (Hampstead/Vaudeville); Mr A's Amazing Maze Plays, Watch On The Rhine, Close of Play (RNT); An Inspector Calls (Theatr Clwyd/Westminster); Dear Charles (Guildford); Hippolytus, Dr. Faustus (London Fringe); Eden End, The Ballroom, The Beaux Stratagem, Man of the Moment, Othello, Taking Steps (Stephen Joseph Theatre, Scarborough); Zero Hour (Edinburgh Fringe); The White Devil (Old Vic).
Television includes: Sword of Honour, Cor Blimey!, The Detectives, Class Act, The Mixer, An Ungentlemanly Act, Twelfth Night, The Bill, Casualty, Moonfleet, A Horseman Riding By, Thomas and Sarah, David.
Radio includes: Les Liaisons Dangereuses, Tales the Countess Told, The Ghost Train, Thrush Green, Forty Years On, Birdsong, My Cousin Rachel.

Barnaby Kay
For the Royal Court: The Man of Mode, The Libertine (co-productions with Out of Joint), Three Sisters, The Break of Day (Out of Joint tour), Trust.
Other theatre includes: The Changeling, A Winter's Tale, The Taming of the Shrew, A Jovial Crew (RSC); Closer (RNT); King of Prussia (Chichester Festival Theatre); The Herbal Bed (RSC/Duchess, West End).
Television includes: The Bill (six episodes), The Castle, Jonathan Creek, Cracker, The Vet, Casualty.
Film includes: The Furnace, Blonde Bombshell, Shakespeare in Love, Oscar and Lucinda, Crucifixion Island, Conspiracy: The Meeting at Wansee.
Radio includes: Crime and Punishment, Moliere, Rites of Passage, Unlike Anyone Else.

Michael Maloney
For the Royal Court: Built on Sand.
Other theatre includes: King Lear, A Woman Killed with Kindness, Romeo and Juliet, Henry IV, Parts 1&2, Derek, Antony and Cleopatra, The Tempest, Lear, The Roaring Girl, Macbeth (RSC); Sleuth (National tour); In the Blue, Alice's Adventures Underground, Once in a While... (RNT); Hamlet (Greenwich, West Yorkshire Playhouse & tour); In Lambeth (Donmar Warehouse); All My Sons (Royal Exchange); Peer Gynt (Cambridge); The London Cuckolds (Lyric Hammersmith); Two Planks and A Passion (Greenwich); The Perfectionist (Hampstead); Can You Hear Me at the Back (Piccadilly); Taking Steps (Lyric).
Television includes: The Swap, A Christmas Carol, The Painted Lady, Macbeth, Sex and Chocolate, The Writing Game, Signs and Wonders, Love on a Branch Line, Trafford Tanzi, Young Indie 'Paris, May 1919', Mr Wakefield's Crusade, Snow, Relatively Speaking, The Lorelei, Starlings, Scoop, The Rivals, Naming the Names, What If Its' Raining, The Bell, Telford's Change, Tartuffe, Last Place on Earth, Living With Dinosaurs.
Film includes: American Reel, Hysteria, Hamlet, Othello, In the Bleak Midwinter, Truly, Madly, Deeply, Henry V, The Mask, Sharma and Beyond, Ordeal by Innocence, Richard's Things, Sans Plomb.

Andrew McKay
Theatre includes: Viva Ibiza (Avondale Theatre, London).
Television includes: Agent Z and the Penguin from Mars, Walking on the Moon, The Bill, London's Burning, Losing It.

Nina Raine (assistant director)
For the Royal Court: Far Away, My Zinc Bed.
Theatre includes: Passion Play, Miss Julie (Burton Taylor Theatre, Oxford); The Way of the World (for the Red Cross at Trebinshwyn); Ashes to Ashes.
Nina is currently on the Regional Theatre Young Director Scheme at the Royal Court Theatre.

Ian Rickson (director)

Ian Rickson is Artistic Director of the Royal Court.

For the Royal Court: Dublin Carol, The Weir (Theatre Upstairs and Theatre Downstairs), The Lights, Pale Horse, Mojo (& Steppenwolf Theatre Co., Chicago), Ashes and Sand, Some Voices, Killers (1992 Young Writers' Festival), Wildfire.

Other theatre includes: The Day I Stood Still (RNT); The House of Yes (The Gate, London): Me and My Friend (Chichester Festival Theatre); Queer Fish (BAC); First Strike (Soho Poly).

Opera includes: La Serva Padrona (Broomhill).

Mark Thompson (designer)

For the Royal Court: Never Land (co-production with The Foundry), Hysteria (and Duke of York's/ Mark Taper Forum, Los Angeles), The Kitchen, Six Degrees of Separation (and Comedy).

Other theatre includes: The Lady in the Van (Queen's); Mamma Mia! (Prince Edward/ Toronto/ U.S. tour); Dr Dolittle (Apollo Hammersmith & UK tour); Blast (Apollo Hammersmith/U.S. tour); Jumpers, The Country Wife, The School for Scandal (Royal Exchange, Manchester); Mumbo Jumbo (Royal Exchange, Manchester/Lyric Hammersmith); Owners (Young Vic); Good (Brussels); The Scarlet Pimpernel (Chichester/Her Majesty's); Cabaret, Ivanov, Much Ado About Nothing (The Strand); The Sneeze (Aldwych); A Little Night Music (Piccadilly); Shadowlands (Queen's & Broadway); Joseph and His Amazing Technicolor Dreamcoat (Palladium/ Canadian, Australian and U.S. tours); The Front Page, Insignificance (Donmar); Company (Donmar & Albery), The Blue Room (Donmar & Broadway); Art (Wyndhams Theatre/U.S./ Australia/Argentina); Measure for Measure, The Wizard of Oz, Much Ado About Nothing, The Comedy of Errors, Hamlet (RSC); The Unexpected Man (RSC/ Fortune/New York); Volpone, Betrayal, Party Time, Butterfly Kiss (Almeida); Life x 3, The Wind in the Willows, The Madness of George III, Pericles, What the Butler Saw, The Day I Stood Still (RNT); Arcadia (RNT/Haymarket/Lincoln Center, New York).

Opera includes: Falstaff (Scottish Opera); Peter Grimes (Opera North), Ariadne Auf Naxos (Salzburg); Il Viaggio A Reims (Royal Opera House); Hansel and Gretel (Sydney Opera House); The Two Widows (ENO); Queen of Spades (The Met, New York), and costume design for Montag Aus Licht (La Scala, Milan).

Ballet includes: Don Quixote (Royal Ballet).

Film includes: The Madness of King George (costume design).

Awards include Olivier Award and critics' Circle Award for Wind in the Willows (1991), Olivier Awards for Set Design and Costume Design for Joseph and The Amazing Technicolor Dreamcoat and The Comedy of Errors. Mark won an Olivier Award in 1994 for Hysteria and a Critics' Circle Award in 1995 for The Kitchen.

Hugh Vanstone (lighting)

Theatre includes: Life x 3, The Cherry Orchard, The Day I Stood Still, The Homecoming (RNT); The Caretaker (Comedy); The Graduate (Gielgud); The Lady In the Van (Queen's Theatre); Blast (Apollo Hammersmith/US tour); Doctor Dolittle (Apollo Hammersmith/UK tour); Orpheus Descending, The Blue Room, Juno and the Paycock, The Front Page, Insignificance (Donmar); Five Kinds of Silence, Mrs Warren's Profession, Moll Flanders (Lyric Hammersmith); The Unexpected Man (RSC/Duchess/Broadway); Closer (RNT/ Lyric/Broadway); Art (Wyndham's Theatre/ U.S./Australia/Argentina); When We Are Married, Copacabana, Scrooge, Once On This Island, Moby Dick (West End); Dance of the Vampires (Vienna/Stuttgart); Peter Pan, Romeo and Juliet (West Yorkshire Playhouse); Miss Julie (Young Vic); Butterfly Kiss (Almeida); Antony and Cleopatra, Bad Weather, Cymbeline, Hamlet (RSC).

Opera includes: Macbeth (Bastille, Paris); The Carmelites, La Boheme (ENO); Carmen (Opera North); The Bartered Bride (Glyndebourne); The Rake's Progress (Welsh National Opera); Die Fledermaus (Scottish Opera).

Ballet inclues: Alice in Wonderland (ENB). Awards include a 1996 Olivier Award nomination for Art, a 1997 Olivier Award nomination for Hamlet, and 1999 Olivier Awards for both The Blue Room and The Unexpected Man.

Peter Wight

For the Royal Court: Not A Game For Boys, Sudlow's Dawn.

Other theatre includes: Sleep With Me, Waiting for Godot, Black Snow, Arturo Ui, Murmuring Judges (RNT); Much Ado About Nothing, Spanish Tragedy, Hamlet, Clockwork Orange, Barbarians (RSC); Edward II (Royal Exchange, Manchester); A Passion in Six Days, Mystery Bouffe, The Nest, Midsummer Night's Dream, Joking Apart (Crucible, Sheffield); King Lear, Three Sisters (Birmingham Rep); The Nose, Hedda Gabler, Risky City (Belgrade, Coventry); Hard to Get (Traverse, Edinburgh); The Seagull, Chekhov's Women (West End); Grace, Dearly Beloved (Hampstead); Othello, Commedia, A State of Affairs, Progress (Lyric Hammersmith); The Caretaker (Globe Theatre Company, Warsaw); The Seagull (Shared Experience).

Television includes: Care, The Blind Date, Active Defence, Our Mutual Friend, Jane Eyre, Wokenwell, Staying Alive, Touch of Frost, The Passion, Out of the Blue, Devil's Advocate, Speaking in Tongues, Meat, Anna Lee, Hearts and Minds, Will You Still Love Me, Yesterday's Dreams, Codename Kyril, The Fourth Floor, Casualty, Exclusive Yarns, Return of the Native.

Film includes: Lucky Break, The Fourth Angel, Shiner, Fairytale, Secret and Lies, Naked, Meantime, Personal Services, A Small Deposit, A Turnip Head's Guide to Alan Parker.

Lucy Whybrow

Theatre includes: Amadeus (West End/tour); Separate Tables (King's Head); An Enemy of the People (RNT); Romeo and Juliet, The Cherry Orchard, The Phoenician Women, Easter (RSC); Arcadia (Haymarket); Celestina (ATC).

Television includes: Shades, Black Cab, The Mill on the Floss, Sherlock Holmes, KYTV.

Film includes: The Biographer, Tenth Kingdom.

Radio includes: The Fox, Dombey and Son, Alice in Wonderland.

AWARDS FOR
THE ROYAL COURT

Ariel Dorfman's Death and the Maiden and John Guare's Six Degrees of Separation won the Olivier Award for Best Play in 1992 and 1993 respectively. Terry Johnson's Hysteria won the 1994 Olivier Award for Best Comedy, and also the Writers' Guild Award for Best West End Play. Kevin Elyot's My Night with Reg won the 1994 Writers' Guild Award for Best Fringe Play, the Evening Standard Award for Best Comedy, and the 1994 Olivier Award for Best Comedy. Joe Penhall was joint winner of the 1994 John Whiting Award for Some Voices. Sebastian Barry won the 1995 Writers' Guild Award for Best Fringe Play, the 1995 Critics' Circle Award and the 1997 Christopher Ewart-Biggs Literary Prize for The Steward of Christendom, and the 1995 Lloyds Private Banking Playwright of the Year Award. Jez Butterworth won the 1995 George Devine Award for Most Promising Playwright, the 1995 Writers' Guild New Writer of the Year Award, the Evening Standard Award for Most Promising Playwright and the 1995 Olivier Award for Best Comedy for Mojo. Phyllis Nagy won the 1995 Writers' Guild Award for Best Regional Play for Disappeared.

The Royal Court won the 1995 Prudential Award for Theatre and was the overall winner of the 1995 Prudential Award for the Arts for creativity, excellence, innovation and accessibility. The Royal Court Theatre Upstairs won the 1995 Peter Brook Empty Space Award for innovation and excellence in theatre.

Michael Wynne won the 1996 Meyer-Whitworth Award for The Knocky. Martin McDonagh won the 1996 George Devine Award, the 1996 Writers' Guild Best Fringe Play Award, the 1996 Critics' Circle Award and the 1996 Evening Standard Award for Most Promising Playwright for The Beauty Queen of Leenane. Marina Carr won the 19th Susan Smith Blackburn Prize (1996/7) for Portia Coughlan. Conor McPherson won the 1997 George Devine Award, the 1997 Critics' Circle Award and the 1997 Evening Standard Award for Most Promising Playwright for The Weir. Ayub Khan-Din won the 1997 Writers' Guild Award for Best West End Play, the 1997 Writers' Guild New Writer of the Year Award and the 1996 John Whiting Award for East is East. Anthony Neilson won the 1997 Writers' Guild Award for Best Fringe Play for The Censor.

At the 1998 Tony Awards, Martin McDonagh's The Beauty Queen of Leenane (co-production with Druid Theatre Company) won four awards including Garry Hynes for Best Director and was nominated for a further two. Eugene Ionesco's The Chairs (co-production with Theatre de Complicite) was nominated for six Tony awards. David Hare won the 1998 Time Out Live Award for Outstanding Achievement and six awards in New York including the Drama League, Drama Desk and New York Critics Circle Award for Via Dolorosa. Sarah Kane won the 1998 Arts Foundation Fellowship in Playwriting. Rebecca Prichard won the 1998 Critics' Circle Award for Most Promising Playwright for Yard Gal.

Conor McPherson won the 1999 Olivier Award for Best New Play for The Weir. The Royal Court won the 1999 ITI Award for Excellence in International Theatre. Sarah Kane's Cleansed was judged Best Foreign Language Play in 1999 by Theater Heute in Germany. Gary Mitchell won the 1999 Pearson Best Play Award for Trust. Rebecca Gilman was joint winner of the 1999 George Devine Award and won the 1999 Evening Standard Award for Most Promising Playwright for The Glory of Living. Roy Williams and Gary Mitchell were joint winners of the George Devine Award 2000 for Most Promising Playwright for Lift Off and The Force of Change respectively. At the Barclays Theatre Awards 2000 presented by the TMA, Richard Wilson won the Best Director Award for David Gieselmann's Mr Kolpert and Jeremy Herbert won the Best Designer Award for Sarah Kane's 4.48 Psychosis. Gary Mitchell won the Evening Standard's Charles Wintour Award 2000 for Most Promising Playwright for The Force of Change. Stephen Jeffreys' I Just Stopped by to See The Man won an AT&T: On Stage Award 2000.

In 1999, the Royal Court won the European theatre prize New Theatrical Realities, presented at Taormina Arte in Sicily, for its efforts in recent years in discovering and producing the work of young British dramatists.

ROYAL COURT BOOKSHOP

The bookshop offers a wide range of playtexts, theatre books, screenplays and art-house videos with over 1,000 titles. Located in the downstairs Bar and Food area, the bookshop is open Monday to Saturday, afternoons and evenings.

Many Royal Court playtexts are available for just £2 including the plays in the current season and recent works by David Hare, Conor McPherson, Martin Crimp, Sarah Kane, David Mamet, Phyllis Nagy, Gary Mitchell, Marina Carr, Martin McDonagh, Ayub Khan-Din, Jim Cartwright and Rebecca Prichard. We offer a 10% reduction to students on a range of titles.
Further information : 020 7565 5024

THE ENGLISH STAGE COMPANY AT THE ROYAL COURT

The English Stage Company at the Royal Court opened in 1956 as a subsidised theatre producing new British plays, international plays and some classical revivals.

The first artistic director George Devine aimed to create a writers' theatre, 'a place where the dramatist is acknowledged as the fundamental creative force in the theatre and where the play is more important than the actors, the director, the designer'. The urgent need was to find a contemporary style in which the play, the acting, direction and design are all combined. He believed that 'the battle will be a long one to continue to create the right conditions for writers to work in'.

Devine aimed to discover 'hard-hitting, uncompromising writers whose plays are stimulating, provocative and exciting'. The Royal Court production of John Osborne's Look Back in Anger in May 1956 is now seen as the decisive starting point of modern British drama, and the policy created a new generation of British playwrights. The first wave included John Osborne, Arnold Wesker, John Arden, Ann Jellicoe, N F Simpson and Edward Bond. Early seasons included new international plays by Bertolt Brecht, Eugène Ionesco, Samuel Beckett, Jean-Paul Sartre and Marguerite Duras.

The theatre started with the 400-seat proscenium arch Theatre Downstairs, and then in 1969 opened a second theatre, the 60-seat studio Theatre Upstairs. Productions in the Theatre Upstairs have transferred to the West End, such as Caryl Churchill's Far Away, Conor McPherson's The Weir, Kevin Elyot's My Night With Reg and Ariel Dorfman's Death and the Maiden. The Royal Court also co-produces plays which have transferred to the West End or toured internationally, such as Sebastian Barry's The Steward of Christendom and Mark Ravenhill's Shopping and Fucking (with Out of Joint), Martin McDonagh's The Beauty Queen Of Leenane (with Druid Theatre Company), Ayub Khan-Din's East is East (with Tamasha Theatre Company, and now a feature film).

Since 1994 the Royal Court's artistic policy has again been vigorously directed to finding and producing a new generation of playwrights. The writers include Joe Penhall, Rebecca Prichard, Michael Wynne, Nick Grosso, Judy Upton, Meredith Oakes, Sarah Kane, Anthony Neilson, Judith Johnson, James Stock, Jez Butterworth, Marina Carr, Simon Block, Martin McDonagh, Mark Ravenhill, Ayub Khan-Din, Tamantha Hammerschlag, Jess Walters, Che Walker, Conor McPherson, Simon Stephens, Richard Bean, Roy

photo: Andy Chopping

Williams, Gary Mitchell, Mick Mahoney, Rebecca Gilman, Christopher Shinn, Kia Corthron, David Gieselmann, Marius von Mayenburg and David Eldridge. This expanded programme of new plays has been made possible through the support of A.S.K Theater Projects, the Jerwood Charitable Foundation, the American Friends of the Royal Court and many in association with the Royal National Theatre Studio.

In recent years there have been record-breaking productions at the box office, with capacity houses for Jez Butterworth's Mojo, Sebastian Barry's The Steward of Christendom, Martin McDonagh's The Beauty Queen of Leenane, Ayub Khan-Din's East is East, Eugène Ionesco's The Chairs, David Hare's My Zinc Bed and Conor McPherson's The Weir, which transferred to the West End in October 1998 and ran for nearly two years at the Duke of York's Theatre.

The newly refurbished theatre in Sloane Square opened in February 2000, with a policy still inspired by the first artistic director George Devine. The Royal Court is an international theatre for new plays and new playwrights, and the work shapes contemporary drama in Britain and overseas.

REBUILDING THE ROYAL COURT

In 1995, the Royal Court was awarded a National Lottery grant through the Arts Council of England, to pay for three quarters of a £26m project to completely rebuild our 100-year old home. The rules of the award required the Royal Court to raise £7.6m in partnership funding. The building has been completed thanks to the generous support of those listed below.

We are particularly grateful for the contributions of over 5,700 audience members.

THE AMERICAN FRIENDS OF THE ROYAL COURT THEATRE

AFRCT support the mission of the Royal Court and are primarily focused on raising funds to enable the theatre to produce new work by emerging American writers. Since this not-for-profit organisation was founded in 1997, AFRCT has contributed to seven productions including Rebecca Gilman's Spinning Into Butter. They have also supported the participation of young artists in the Royal Court's acclaimed International Residency.

If you would like to support the ongoing work of the Royal Court, please contact the Development Department on 020 7565 5050.

ROYAL COURT
DEVELOPMENT BOARD
Elisabeth Murdoch (Chair)
Jonathan Cameron (Vice Chair)
Timothy Burrill
Anthony Burton
Jonathan Caplan QC
Joyce Hytner
Dany Khosrovani
Feona McEwan
Michael Potter
Sue Stapely
Charlotte Watcyn Lewis

PRINCIPAL DONOR
Jerwood Foundation

WRITERS CIRCLE
The Cadogan Estate
Carillon/Schal
News International plc
Pathé
The Eva and Hans K Rausing Trust
The Rayne Foundation
Sky
Garfield Weston Foundation

DIRECTORS CIRCLE
The Esmée Fairbairn Charitable Trust
The Granada Group plc

ACTORS CIRCLE
Edward C Cohen & The Blessing Way Foundation
Ronald Cohen & Sharon Harel-Cohen
Quercus Charitable Trust
The Basil Samuel Charitable Trust
The Trusthouse Charitable Foundation
The Woodward Charitable Trust

SPECIFIC DONATIONS
The Foundation for Sport and the Arts for Stage System
John Lewis Partnership plc for Balcony
City Parochial Foundation for Infra Red Induction Loops and Toilets for Disabled Patrons
RSA Art for Architecture Award Scheme for Antoni Malinowski Wall Painting

AMERICAN FRIENDS

Founders
Harry Brown
Victoria Elenowitz
Francis Finlay
Monica Gerard-Sharp
The Howard Gilman Foundation
Jeananne Hauswald
Mary Ellen Johnson
Dany Khosrovani
Kay Koplovitz
The Laura Pels Foundation
Stephen Magowan
Monica Menell-Kinberg Ph.D.
Benjamin Rauch
Rory Riggs
Robert Rosenkranz
Gerald Schoenfeld, The Shubert Organization

Patrons
Daniel Baudendistel
Arthur Bellinzoni
Miriam Bienstock
Robert L & Janice Billingsley
Catherine G Curran
Leni Darrow
Michael & Linda Donovan
Ursula & William Fairbairn
April Foley
Amanda Foreman
Mr & Mrs Richard Gelfond
Mr & Mrs Richard Grand
Mr & Mrs Paul Hallingby
Sharon King Hoge
The Carl C Icahn Family Foundation
Maurice & Jean R Jacobs
Mr & Mrs Ernest Kafka
Sahra T Lese
Susan & Martin Lipton
Eleanor Margolis
Hamish & Georgone Maxwell
Kathleen O'Grady
Howard & Barbara Sloan
Margaret Jackson Smith
Mika Sterling
Arielle Tepper
The Thorne Foundation

Benefactors
Mr & Mrs Tom Armstrong
Mr & Mrs Mark Arnold
Elaine Attias
Rachael Bail
Mr & Mrs Matthew Chapman
David Day
Richard & Rosalind Edelman
Abe & Florence Elenowitz
Hiram & Barbara Gordon
Mr & Mrs Brian Keelan
Jennifer C E Laing
Burt Lerner
Imelda Liddiard
Dr Anne Locksley
Mr & Mrs Rudolph Rauch
Lawrence & Helen Remmel
Mr & Mrs Robert Rosenberg
Mr & Mrs William Russell
Harold Sanditen
Mr & Mrs Robert Scully
Julie Talen
Mr & Mrs Charles Whitman

THE
ARTS
COUNCIL
OF ENGLAND

PROGRAMME SUPPORTERS

The Royal Court (English Stage Company Ltd) receives its principal funding from London Arts. It is also supported financially by a wide range of private companies and public bodies and earns the remainder of its income from the box office and its own trading activities.

The Royal Borough of Kensington & Chelsea gives an annual grant to the Royal Court Young Writers' Programme and the London Boroughs Grants Committee provides project funding for a number of play development initiatives.

Royal Court Registered Charity number 231242.

The Jerwood Charitable Foundation continues to support new plays by new playwrights with the series of Jerwood New Playwrights. Since 1993 the A.S.K. Theater Projects of Los Angeles has funded a Playwrights' Programme at the theatre. Bloomberg Mondays, a continuation of the Royal Court's reduced price ticket scheme, is supported by Bloomberg. Sky has also generously committed to a two-year sponsorship of the Royal Court Young Writers' Festival.

Recently Stage Hands donors, who are members of the Royal Court audience, supported three plays: My Zinc Bed by David Hare, Far Away by Caryl Churchill and I Just Stopped By to See The Man by Stephen Jeffreys.

TRUSTS AND FOUNDATIONS
American Friends of the Royal Court Theatre
Carlton Television Trust
Gerald Chapman Fund
Cultural Foundation Deutsche Bank
The Genesis Foundation
The Goldsmiths Company
Jerwood Charitable Foundation
The John Lyons Charity
Laura Pels Foundation
Quercus Charitable Trust
The Peggy Ramsay Foundation
The Peter Sharp Foundation
Royal Victoria Hall Foundation
The Trusthouse Charitable Foundation

MAJOR SPONSORS
A.S.K. Theater Projects
AT&T
Barclays plc
Bloomberg
Sky
Credit Suisse First Boston
Francis Finlay
Lever Fabergé (through Arts & Business New Partners)
Royal College of Psychiatrists

BUSINESS MEMBERS
Goldman Sachs International
Laporte plc
Lazard Brothers & Co. Ltd
Lever Fabergé
McCABES
Redwood Publishing
Simons Muirhead & Burton
J Walter Thompson

INDIVIDUAL MEMBERS
Patrons
David H Adams
Advanpress
Katie Bradford

Mrs Alan Campbell-Johnson
Gill Carrick
Chris Corbin
David Day
Greg Dyke
Thomas Fenton
Ralph A Fields
John Flower
Mike Frain
Edna & Peter Goldstein
Judy & Frank Grace
David Graham
Phil Hobbs
Homevale Ltd
JHJ & SF Lewis
Lex Service plc
Barbara Minto
Michael & Mimi Naughton
New Penny Productions Ltd
Martin Newson
AT Poeton & Son Ltd.
André Ptaszynski, Really Useful Theatres
David Rowland
Sir George Russell
Bernard Shapero
Carl & Martha Tack
Mr & Mrs Anthony Weldon
Richard Wilson
George & Moira Yip

Benefactors
Anastasia Alexander
Lesley E Alexander
Batia Asher
Elaine Mitchell Attias
Thomas Bendhem
Jody Berger
Keith & Helen Bolderson
Jeremy Bond
Mr & Mrs F H Bradley III
Mrs Elly Brook JP
Julian Brookstone
Debbi & Richard Burston
Yuen-Wei Chew
Carole & Neville Conrad
Conway Van Gelder
Coppard & Co.

Barry Cox
Curtis Brown Ltd
Deborah Davis
Zöe Dominic
Robyn Durie
Lorraine Esdaile
Winston & Jean Fletcher
Claire & William Frankel
Nicholas Fraser
Robert Freeman
J Garcia
Beverley & Nathaniel Gee
Norman Gerard
Henny Gestetner OBE
Jacqueline & Jonathan Gestetner
Michael Goddard
Carolyn Goldbart
Sally Greene
Byron Grote
Sue & Don Guiney
Hamilton Asper Management
Anna Home CBE
Amanda Howard Associates
ICM Ltd
Trevor Ingman
Lisa Irwin-Burgess
Peter Jones
Paul Kaju & Jane Peterson
Peter & Maria Kellner
Diana King
Clico Kingsbury
Lee & Thompson
CA Leng
Lady Lever
Colette & Peter Levy
Ian Mankin
Christopher Marcus
Nicola McFarland
James McIvor
Mr & Mrs Roderick R McManigal
Mae Modiano
Eva Monley
Pat Morton
Georgia Oetker
Paul Oppenheimer

Mr & Mrs Michael Orr
Maria Peacock
Pauline Pinder
Carol Rayman
Angharad Rees
John & Rosemarie Reynolds
John Ritchie
Bernice & Victor Sandelson
John Sandoe (Books) Ltd
Nicholas Selmes
Lois Sieff OBE
Peregrine Simon
David & Patricia Smalley
Brian D Smith
John Soderquist
Max Stafford-Clark
Sue Stapely
Ann Marie Starr
Anthony Wigram

STAGE HANDS CIRCLE
Graham Billing
Andrew Cryer
Lindy Fletcher
Mr R Hopkins
Philip Hughes Trust
Dr A V Jones
Roger Jospe
Miss A Lind-Smith
Mr J Mills
Nevin Charitable Trust
Jeremy Priestley
Ann Scurfield
Brian Smith
Harry Streets
C C Wright

FOR THE ROYAL COURT

Royal Court Theatre
Sloane Square, London SW1W 8AS
Tel: 020 7565 5050 Fax: 020 7565 5001
info@royalcourttheatre.com
www.royalcourttheatre.com

ARTISTIC
Artistic Director **Ian Rickson**
Assistant to the Artistic Director **Jo Luke**
Associate Director **Dominic Cooke**
Associate Director International **Elyse Dodgson**
Associate Director Casting **Lisa Makin**
Associate Directors* **Stephen Daldry, James Macdonald, Katie Mitchell, Max Stafford-Clark, Richard Wilson**
Literary Manager **Graham Whybrow**
Literary Associate **Stephen Jeffreys***
Voice Associate **Patsy Rodenburg***
Casting Assistant **Amy Ball**
International Administrator **Natalie Highwood**
International Associate **Ramin Gray** +
Trainee Director (RTYDS) **Nina Raine** §

YOUNG WRITERS' PROGRAMME
Associate Director **Ola Animashawun**
General Manager **Aoife Mannix**
Education Officer **Christine Hope**
Outreach Worker **Lucy Dunkerley**
Writers' Tutor **Simon Stephens***

PRODUCTION
Production Manager **Paul Handley**
Deputy Production Manager **Sue Bird**
Facilities Manager **Fran McElroy**
Maintenance Deputy **Robert Goacher**
Production Assistant **Jane Ashfield**
Company Stage Manager **Cath Binks**
Head of Lighting **Johanna Town**
Lighting Deputy **Marion Mahon**
Assistant Electrician **Heidi Riley, Gavin Owen**
Lighting Board Operator TD **Andrew Taylor**
Head of Stage **Martin Riley**
Stage Deputy **David Berry**
Stage Chargehand **Davey McCusker**
Head of Sound **Paul Arditti**
Sound Deputy **Ian Dickinson**
Head of Wardrobe **Iona Kenrick**
Wardrobe Deputy **Suzanne Duffy**

MANAGEMENT
Executive Director **Vikki Heywood**
Assistant to the Executive Director **Lyn Edwards**
General Manager **Diane Borger**
Finance Director **Sarah Preece**
Finance Officer **Rachel Harrison**
Re-development Finance Officer **Neville Ayres**
Finance Assistant **Martin Wheeler**

MARKETING & PRESS
Head of Marketing **Penny Mills**
Head of Press **Giselle Glasman**
Marketing Officer **Emily Smith**
Marketing and Press Assistant **Claire Christou**
Box Office Manager **Neil Grutchfield**
Deputy Box Office Manager **Valli Dakshinamurthi**
Duty Box Office Manager **Glen Bowman**
Box Office Sales Operators **Carol Pritchard, Steven Kuleshnyk**

DEVELOPMENT
Head of Development **Helen Salmon**
Development Associate **Susan Davenport** *
Sponsorship Manager **Rebecca Preston**
Development Assistant **SJ Griffin**

FRONT OF HOUSE
Theatre Manager **Elizabeth Brown**
Deputy Theatre Manager **Grainne Cook**
Duty House Managers **Neil Morris*, Teresa Dray*, Jo Luke***
Bookshop Assistant **Teresa Munafo***
Stage Door/Reception **Simon David, Adam Griffiths*, Andrew Mcloughlin, Tyrone Lucas.**
Thanks to all of our ushers

* part-time
+ Arts Council International Associate
§ This theatre has the support of The Jerwood Charitable Foundation under the Regional Theatre Young Director Scheme, administered by Channel 4 Television.

ENGLISH STAGE COMPANY
Vice Presidents
Jocelyn Herbert
Joan Plowright CBE
Council
Chairman **Sir John Mortimer QC, CBE**
Vice-Chairman **Anthony Burton**
Members
Stuart Burge CBE
Martin Crimp
Judy Daish
Stephen Evans
Phyllida Lloyd
Sonia Melchett
James Midgley
Richard Pulford
Hugh Quarshie
Nicholas Wright
Alan Yentob

Honorary Council
Sir Richard Eyre
Alan Grieve

Advisory Council
Diana Bliss
Tina Brown
Allan Davis
Elyse Dodgson
Robert Fox
Jocelyn Herbert
Michael Hoffman
Hanif Kureishi
Jane Rayne
Ruth Rogers
James L. Tanner

The Bush Theatre presents
The Red Room and Mama Quillo's
production of

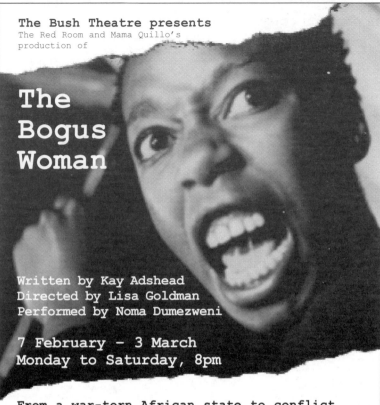

The
Bogus
Woman

Written by Kay Adshead
Directed by Lisa Goldman
Performed by Noma Dumezweni

7 February – 3 March
Monday to Saturday, 8pm

From a war-torn African state to conflict
in a British detention centre, one asylum
seeker tells her story...

"Powerful, passionate and
committed. If I were Greg
Dyke, I would put it straight
on BBC TV and invite Jack
Straw to respond"
Michael Billington
The Guardian

"Kay Adshead's angry,
stripped-down script bleeds
humanity. Solo performer Noma
Dumezweni is mesmerising in
the spotlight"
The Independent

Fringe First Winner
Edinburgh 2000

Tickets
Monday – Thursday £12 (£8 concessions)
Friday & Saturday £13 (£8.50 concessions)

Box Office 020 7610 4224

The Bush Theatre, Shepherds Bush Green,
London W12 8QD

the
R E D
ROOM

thebushtheatre

MOUTH TO MOUTH

Kevin Elyot

For my mother

*The whole art of living is to make use
of the individuals through whom we suffer.*

Proust

6

Characters

FRANK, ~~46~~ *43*

LAURA, ~~45~~ *42*

GOMPERTZ, *35*

DENNIS, *43*

PHILLIP, ~~15~~ */17*

CORNELIA, ~~28~~ *25*

ROGER, *34*

The action takes place in a house and a restaurant.

At the time of going to press, rehearsals were not completed, so the text here may differ from that in performance

A tango. Lights up on:

The Kitchen

FRANK *and* LAURA *sit by the open French windows which look out onto the garden. Adjoining the kitchen is a pantry, also in view. Sunlight streams in.* FRANK *has a huge bandage over his left eye.* LAURA*'s wearing sunglasses. She's smoking. The tango music cross-fades with the sounds of summer gardens: the steady rhythm of a sprinkler system, an intermittent distant strimmer, children playing and birdsong. Also, from another part of the house, we hear a piano: a faltering rendition of the Aria from Bach's Goldberg Variations.*

FRANK. . . . so I'm – I'm having it off tomorrow.

Beat.

They said it should do the trick, but I might have to have another put in; depends if I keep taking the tablets. We'll see. It's so lovely here.

He lifts his face to the sun.

You could almost forget you're in Balham.

For a moment he's distracted by something in the garden. LAURA *looks at him. He returns his attention.*

It was odd, I must say, walking into the operating theatre. I mean, you don't usually do that, do you? Usually you're wheeled in totally out of it, but I just walked in totally *compos mentis.* Of course, once it had started, I didn't have a clue what was going on. She asked if I was okay, but I was concentrating so hard on not panicking, I don't think I answered, and the only time she told me what was happening was when she put it in and stitched it up, then it was over. Incredible, isn't it? You drop in after breakfast

and you're home by lunchtime. (*Re. the garden*). I'm sure
someone . . .

Beat.

What I can't work out is whether or not she popped the
eyeball out of its socket. The thought of lying there with
one of my eyes dangling on my cheek . . . It's no good, you
know. I was given the impression it was going to be alright,
but I can tell by the way they are with me that it's not quite
going according to plan.

LAURA *squeezes his hand.*

Funny how things turn out, isn't it? We thought it was just
going to fall into our laps.

Beat.

Laura . . .

*She looks at him. Beat. He kisses her hand. They gaze out at
the garden.*

God, I need this break and if it doesn't work out, well . . .

Beat.

I had dinner with my doctor last night. It's quite nice really
how we've sort of meandered into a friendship. He thinks
I'm mad. He says it's just a blip. I mean, I'd put up with it
all if I was sure it was working: the bad dreams, the way I
look – but no, I've had enough. Tantamount to suicide
according to Doctor Gompertz, but I look at it as a way of
taking control.

LAURA *lights another cigarette from the one she's
smoking.*

You'll miss this place, won't you? Anyway . . .

Beat.

He does go on. He lost his partner ages ago now, but he
always comes back to it. Gets himself into such a state,
especially when he's had a few, and I never got round to
talking about –

Pause.

Well, there was something – that I particularly wanted to talk about which is why I'd arranged to meet him in the first place, and I – I never got round to it.

He's distracted again by something in the garden.

Look, down the bottom there, I'm sure . . . Probably just a shadow. I thought – for a second, I thought it was –

The kitchen-table suddenly shifts about a foot. He leaps to his feet and stares at it. LAURA tenses.

Jesus!

Pause.

Better be off.

She looks at him.

. . . In a bit.

He sits down again.

Laura, there's something –

The sound of a motorbike approaching. They freeze. The piano stops. The bike gets closer. LAURA starts to remove her glasses. Blackout as the bike gets louder. It cuts out as the lights snap up on:

A Restaurant

FRANK *and* GOMPERTZ *at a table. They have drinks and menus.* FRANK *has the dressing over his left eye.* GOMPERTZ *has his face in his napkin. He lets out an involuntary sob.* FRANK *is acutely embarrassed.*

GOMPERTZ. Sorry . . .

FRANK. No, no, it's . . .

GOMPERTZ. Sorry . . .

FRANK. No . . .

GOMPERTZ *wipes his eyes and face with the napkin, then takes a slug of his drink.*

GOMPERTZ. See, people don't have time to remember, don't even care to remember, but I do. I still can't believe it. The blink of an eyelid and life's changed forever. What's the fucking point! Sorry, you were saying . . .

He lights a cigarette.

FRANK. About the bad dreams. Last night, for example, I dreamt Alan Rickman was being fried for charity.

GOMPERTZ. He was in here last week.

FRANK. And a few nights ago I turned over in bed and Dennis Neilsen was lying next to me; a dream, but nonetheless –

GOMPERTZ. The truth is, when it comes down to it, I just don't trust people. I don't believe a word they say. When I think of his memorial, all the speeches, the pieces and poems, the commiserations and the promises to keep in touch – all crap, isn't it? Self, self, fucking self! (*Re. menu.*) Ooh, Cuttlefish Mousse. Mind you, there've been so many sodding memorials these past years –

FRANK. Isn't that what you feed budgies?

GOMPERTZ. It's a joke. Unknown at birth, forgotten when you're dead, and a load of bollocks in between. Life's a cunt and no mistake. Baryshnikov.

FRANK. What?

GOMPERTZ *nods in the appropriate direction.*

Oh, yes.

GOMPERTZ. Forever alone, that's our lot, and try as we might, we can't change it. We hitch up with someone, fool ourselves we've cracked it, give life to other desolate beings, but we're still alone.

FRANK. This is a real treat. Thanks ever so much.

GOMPERTZ. I mean, look at us: conglomerations of meat and juices tarted up in Armani. And where do we all end up? In a mass of stinking putrefaction. (*Winking and smiling at someone.*) Hi.

FRANK. So tell me, what was it that attracted you to medicine?

GOMPERTZ. The glamour. How's the eye?

FRANK. Fine.

He sips his drink, but misses his mouth.

GOMPERTZ. Kipper Soufflé with Cornichon and Sun-blush Tomato Salsa . . .

FRANK (*wiping the spilt drink with his napkin*). Peter, would she actually have taken my eye out of its socket? I mean, would it have just been hanging on my cheek?

GOMPERTZ. And that sense of being in control.

FRANK. Control. Yes, that's kind of what I wanted to talk to you about.

GOMPERTZ (*indicating with a nod*). Pinter.

FRANK (*looking round*). Oh, yes.

GOMPERTZ. And look who he's with. Intriguing. Carry on.

FRANK. What?

GOMPERTZ. Your dreams.

FRANK. Oh, right. The dreams. Well, I suppose I could just about cope with those, but it's everything else: the diarrhoea, the nausea, headaches, the incessant pill-taking and needles, and most of all, the way my body's changing shape. I used to have quite a decent body, but now I'm like something out of *The Bridge on the River Kwai* : my limbs are like twigs, my neck's like a turkey's, and my bum hangs from my back like a pair of old curtains in a caravan. It's getting me down. I can't bear to look in the mirror anymore. (*Indicating his eye bandage.*) And if this can happen when I'm on medication –

GOMPERTZ. It's a blip, I've told you, just a blip.

FRANK. And it's not just the medication. I need to get away. I need a change of routine.

GOMPERTZ. Sardine Saltimbocca and Dwarf Corn Mulch . . .

FRANK. And I really want to get on with my writing. You know, sometimes I think that's more important to me than my health. Does that sound crazy?

GOMPERTZ (*indicating with a nod*). See that busboy.

FRANK. What?

GOMPERTZ. Lets you snort a line off his stiffy in the lav.

FRANK. Gosh.

GOMPERTZ. Not too pricey either, dirty bitch.

FRANK. Anyway the point is –

   GOMPERTZ *suddenly lets out a sob.*

   Oh dear.

GOMPERTZ. Sorry . . .

FRANK. No, no . . .

GOMPERTZ. It's just – the busboy, as in – walking under one.

FRANK. Ah.

GOMPERTZ. Bloody typical! He didn't even die of the fucking thing that was meant to kill him. (*Taking something from his pocket.*) Run down by a 134 –

FRANK. I know –

GOMPERTZ. – and such a poetic soul!

   It's a cocaine inhaler. He takes a discreet snort.

FRANK. Yes –

GOMPERTZ. Sorry, what were you saying?

FRANK. I've got a bit lost.

GOMPERTZ. Something about writing.

FRANK. Oh, yes. Well, you know I've been blocked for God knows how long.

GOMPERTZ. What a way to go!

FRANK. The point is, I think at last I might have an idea, which in a roundabout way is also what I wanted to talk to you about.

GOMPERTZ *passes the inhaler to* FRANK.

Oh. Thank you.

He awkwardly attempts a snort.

GOMPERTZ. Battered Boudin on Sweet Cicely Coulis? Chef must be shooting up again. Suppose I'll go for the shank of sodding lamb.

He takes another slug of his drink.

All that struggle and angst, worries about money, arguing about whether to go to Polynesia or New England, wondering what colour to paint the gazebo, then nothing. And we were getting on so well. No sex, of course – we went outside the relationship for that. And the mash, I suppose. I'm always having the fucking mash. I think it's best, don't you? –

FRANK. I like a nice mash –

GOMPERTZ. – not having sex with your partner. It makes things so much easier. Of course, we had sex at the beginning, but when you start falling asleep in the middle of it, time to call it a day, eh?

FRANK (*handing back the inhaler*). I suppose so. Peter, there's something –

GOMPERTZ. How the fuck can you not see a bus? He wasn't wearing his glasses, of course – vain little queen – but a bright red double-decker!

He snorts.

He wasn't that blind. God, I miss him! Sometimes, you know, and it's usually when I'm sober, I'm convinced he's around. Like I can smell his scent, follow it across a room, or just sense him at my shoulder. It's nice . . . You've never lived with anyone, have you?

FRANK. Not in a romantic way. But funnily enough that's also sort of tied up with what I wanted to talk to you about.

GOMPERTZ. Do you think we should have a shag?

FRANK. No.

GOMPERTZ. Best not. You were saying . . .

He lights another cigarette.

FRANK. I saved someone's life, you know –

He suddenly winces and holds his stomach.

GOMPERTZ. Alright?

After a moment:

FRANK. Mm.

GOMPERTZ. Of course there's still a combination you haven't tried.

FRANK. There probably is, but what I'm trying to tell you –

GOMPERTZ (*re. someone passing*). Prada suit and a baseball cap? Please!

FRANK. – one of the things I'm trying to tell you – is that I've had enough, and so I've decided – after careful consideration, I have decided . . .

GOMPERTZ. Yes?

FRANK. . . . to stop my medication.

GOMPERTZ is suddenly still; for the first time FRANK has his full attention.

You have to understand, it wears you down after a while. You try something, it works, then it doesn't and your test results go pear-shaped. You try something else, it may work, it may not, and so it goes on. And before each check-up, wondering if your tests are alright, and if they're not, then what? I want to be free of all this, at least for a while, and also give my body a rest from all the poison I've been pumping into it.

GOMPERTZ *hands him the inhaler.*

Thank you.

He takes a discreet snort, GOMPERTZ *watching him.*

So . . . what do you think?

GOMPERTZ. What would you like me to think?

FRANK. You must have an opinion.

GOMPERTZ. Why?

FRANK. You're a doctor.

GOMPERTZ. It's your choice.

FRANK. Peter –

GOMPERTZ. If that's what you want . . . I must say, I'm surprised. We've monitored you with the greatest care for the past several years, prescribed the best and latest treatments. I wouldn't be so crass as to mention what that's cost, but the good thing is that, after all this time, you're still here to tell me you want to give it all up and, as I say, it's your choice.

FRANK. Look –

GOMPERTZ. It's strange because you've always been so co-operative. I expect this from younger guys, but not from people your age. You can remember what it was like, and putting up with a bit of discomfort –

FRANK. A bit!

GOMPERTZ. – is surely preferable to falling off your fucking perch, but if you've developed a death wish, fine. As I say, it's your choice.

FRANK. I can always start up again if things get dodgy.

GOMPERTZ. It doesn't work like that and you know it. Now let me tell *you* something: there was this guy I was treating, about your age, and one day he said exactly what you've just said and, try as I might, I could not make him see sense –

FRANK. Peter, there's something else –

GOMPERTZ. – so he went ahead, gave up all his medication, even wrote an article in one of those mindless radical rags about how the doctors were poisoning their patients –

FRANK. There's something else –

GOMPERTZ. – and within a matter of months he was back on the ward with dementia, and in no time at all –

FRANK. Peter, will you please listen!

Beat.

Sorry. The thing is, there's something else – on my mind. In fact it's driving me mad and I haven't been able to talk to anyone about it.

Beat.

About a year ago, almost to the day, something happened, a dreadful thing, and I don't know for sure whether or not it was my fault. In fact I don't think I'll ever know, and I feel so guilty, I can't bear it anymore, which is one of the reasons why – well, why I need a bit of a break.

GOMPERTZ. We all have our secrets.

FRANK. You see, I've got this friend – Laura – and she . . .

GOMPERTZ. Yes?

FRANK. She had a do – about a year ago, as I said, and –

The bleep of a pager.

GOMPERTZ. Arseholes!

He takes a pager out of his pocket and reads the message.

Wouldn't you know it!

As he gets out his mobile and dials:

Just when we were getting to the interesting bit.

FRANK. Anyway . . .

GOMPERTZ. Sorry. (*Into his mobile.*) Hi, Crippen here . . .
Yes . . . Mm . . .

The tango strikes up as the lights fade. Lights up on:

The Sitting-Room

The music fades. LAURA *is putting out nibbles, plumping
cushions and generally tidying,* DENNIS *is putting on a tie
and* FRANK *is having a drink. He isn't wearing an eye
bandage.*

LAURA. How could you do this? It's Phillip's night and you
have to invite them.

DENNIS. I didn't exactly invite them –

LAURA. Typical of Roger; he has you round his little finger.

DENNIS. They're passing through – what could I do?

LAURA. You could've said no and suggested another night.

DENNIS. This is the only night they're free.

LAURA. And this is a night we're not free.

DENNIS. I thought you might be quite pleased to see them –

LAURA. I'm sure Frank doesn't want to hear you going on
and on about this. (*To* FRANK.) How's your drink?

FRANK. It's –

LAURA. Have an olive. They're Sicilian. (*To* DENNIS.) Why
you didn't leave the machine on –

DENNIS. He's my brother. I haven't seen him for five years.

LAURA. And if you don't phone Abdullah's soon, they won't
be able to get us all in.(*Re. the tie.*) You're not wearing that,
are you?

DENNIS. Roger and Cornelia sent it me last Christmas.

LAURA. I am not going out with you with boomerangs hanging from your throat.

DENNIS glances at FRANK, eyes to heaven. As he goes out:

(*To* FRANK.) Don't you adore this?

She opens a fan with a flick of her wrist.

Phillip bought it for me in Madrid. I think I'll take it to the restaurant; it can get awfully sweaty on a Friday night.

FRANK. Where is Phillip?

LAURA. He's supposed to be in the shower, but he's probably still asleep. He looked like shit when I picked him up from the airport. (*Calling through a door.*) Darling, they'll be here in a sec.

A grunt from a distant part of the house.

God knows what he's been up to! Little Sanchez – that's his penfriend – is such a gentle, mousey thing, not Phillip's style at all. In fact when he stayed here, he was so nice, he bored me to death. But I'm sure they've been up to something. Every time I phoned him, they seemed to have been to the Prado. I know it's big, but please! The good thing is that Señor Morales – that's Sanchez's father – said his Spanish had improved no end. Almost as good as his French, thanks to you.

FRANK. He's a bright boy.

LAURA. I don't know who he gets it from. I was never that hot academically.

FRANK. Maybe he gets it from his Dad.

She snorts.

LAURA (*taking his glass*). Top up?

FRANK. So tell me about Cornelia.

LAURA. She's utterly irritating. I can't stand her. I suppose she's quite pretty in a predictable sort of way, which is why

Roger hitched up with her no doubt, but if you didn't know
otherwise, you'd think she probably worked on the bread
counter at Kwik Save. The fact that she's a rather hot
interior designer wouldn't enter your head. Apparently she
picked up loads of commissions while they were in
Australia.

FRANK. I thought she did something academic.

LAURA. She's taken up Anglo Saxon as a hobby. Can you
imagine? It makes me quite nauseous. And now she's
pregnant after many years of trying, so brace yourself for a
lot of expectant-mother chat. And Roger! Well, I just want
to slap him, he's so puerile. Obviously got away with
murder as the baby of the family. He makes Phillip seem
quite mature.

FRANK. Ah well, Phillip –

LAURA. What do you mean, 'Ah well, Phillip?'

FRANK. Well, I mean . . . well –

LAURA. I am not saying that he's a paragon, but when one
looks at the male influences in his life –

FRANK. Thank you!

LAURA. I don't mean you, and you know it. God above, if it
weren't for you . . . !

She gives him a quick hug and kiss.

No, I am referring to the other men in his life.

FRANK. You're very hard on Dennis.

LAURA. He can be hard on me; he's just quieter about it. I'm
so pleased Phillip's back. When it's just the two of us, we
seem to row more. It's a miracle we don't kill each other.

FRANK. You can't row all the time.

LAURA. When we're not sulking we are, but the sulking
doesn't last because we have to get on to the next row.
You're better off single, I tell you. Oh God!

She's suddenly still.

I hate the way I sound sometimes. When I think of how I've let things slip! I'm forty-five and what have I got to show for it? I've done nothing that I meant to do. I haven't even started. I'm just a mother, and that's about it.

FRANK. That's important.

LAURA. It's not enough.

FRANK. Anyway you're always doing things. You never seem to stop.

LAURA. I know, I know. I have my classes, the choir, the garden, this committee, that committee, but what's it amount to? It doesn't make me feel any better. Oh, I'm sorry, going on and on, as if you haven't got enough on your plate. Tell me about you. Are you well? You look well. And your writing. Tell me about that.

FRANK. Well, it isn't quite coming together at the moment –

LAURA. Have I always been like this? Maybe I have. What an awful thought! No, I don't think so. I think I've changed, haven't I? Or maybe I haven't. No, I'm sure I used to be happy. Or maybe I wasn't. I don't know. Do you think I've changed? If it weren't for Phillip, I'd go mad. Sorry, you were saying . . .

FRANK. It doesn't matter.

LAURA. Yes, it does. Your writing. Tell me.

FRANK. I'm finding it pretty difficult, to be honest. I can't put my finger on why exactly –

LAURA. No ideas.

FRANK. That could be it. But no, I'm having quite a hard time. I'm always being accused of writing about the same thing.

LAURA. And what would that be?

FRANK. Well, me, as it happens, which simply isn't true. They say it's a sign of creative bankruptcy.

LAURA. I'd have thought personal experience was the only thing worth writing about.

FRANK. But my life isn't that interesting, and if it were, I wouldn't have the time to write about it.

LAURA. Oh, I do wish tonight weren't happening!

FRANK. Yes, well . . . Nice olives.

LAURA. You're right, you know: I am hard on Dennis. Perhaps we're just too used to each other.

FRANK. Could be.

LAURA. I'm lucky to have him, I suppose – in a way. He's a kind man, don't you think?

FRANK. He is.

LAURA. And he's been quite good to me, hasn't he?

FRANK. Yes, he has.

LAURA. Always there to – fall back on. Comfy, somehow – like a beanbag. (*She flicks open the fan.*) This is the loveliest . . . I'm going to leave him, you know.

FRANK. You've been saying that for years.

LAURA. But this time I mean it. When Phillip's finished A-levels . . .

PHILLIP has appeared in the doorway, dishevelled, in boxer shorts.

Darling! You're not going out like that, are you?

PHILLIP. I'm knackered.

LAURA. Come here and give your mother a big hug.

He ambles over and she embraces him.

Ah! My angel! Have you missed me?

PHILLIP. Yeah.

LAURA. You horror! I bet you didn't think of me once.

FRANK. Hello, Phillip.

PHILLIP. Hi.

FRANK. Had a good time?

PHILLIP. Yeah.

LAURA. You've grown so much. (*To* FRANK.) Don't you think he's grown?

PHILLIP. I've only been gone a few weeks.

LAURA. You're not my little boy anymore.

PHILLIP. Mum!

The sound of a motorbike approaching.

LAURA. I bet that's them.

PHILLIP. Has Roger got a motorbike?

LAURA. Apparently.

PHILLIP. Brilliant!

LAURA. He probably fancies himself as Brando or James Dean. It's absolutely pathetic.

The bike gets closer.

Darling, clothes.

And closer.

Dennis!

Blackout as the bike gets ever louder. It cuts out as the lights snap up on:

The Sitting-Room

LAURA, DENNIS, PHILLIP, FRANK, ROGER *and* CORNELIA, *three months gone, with drinks and nibbles.* CORNELIA *has a carrier bag at her feet.* PHILLIP *has a packet of photographs.*

CORNELIA. 'What is the point,' I said, 'of having tulipwood shelving around your bath if you're going to deface it with bottles of Asda shampoo and conditioner?' Toiletries tell you so much about a person, don't you think, Laura?

LAURA. Do they?

CORNELIA. Oh, yes.

LAURA. Well, there you go.

DENNIS. So you'll be in Edinburgh for the birth.

CORNELIA. Yes. Our own little bairn. I'm so excited.

ROGER. Finally hit the bull's eye.

LAURA. There's a small Moroccan round the corner.

ROGER. Hear that, Frank?

LAURA. You all like cous-cous, don't you?

CORNELIA. Oh yes, we love it, don't we, Roger?

ROGER (*to* FRANK). You knew Laura when she was a girl, did you?

FRANK. Not quite that far back.

ROGER. Pity. I was hoping you'd give me a blow-by-blow of what she looked like in a gymslip and navy blue knickers. Do you know, Phil, I was only a year older than you are now when I first met your Mum?

PHILLIP. Oh.

ROGER. Yeah. A succulent seventeen-year-old, barely out of short trousers, never been kissed.

DENNIS. Never been kissed!

CORNELIA (*getting something from the carrier bag*). So I'd only have been eleven when you got married, Laura. Just imagine!

LAURA. Yes.

CORNELIA (*handing* LAURA *an oddly shaped parcel*). This is for you.

LAURA. Oh. Thank you.

CORNELIA. Well, for all of you really. A little Australian memento.

LAURA unwraps it. It's an abstract wood carving.

LAURA. It's . . .

CORNELIA. Aboriginal.

LAURA. Yes.

CORNELIA. We think it might be Gumbaingari, but we're not sure. And we think it's called 'The Kiss', but we're not sure of that either.

LAURA. Well, it's . . . nice, whatever.

She hands it to DENNIS.

CORNELIA. The Aborigines are so fascinating, aren't they, Roger? And they do these wonderful paintings and things about animals and this and that and dreamtime and what-have-you.

PHILLIP. We've got an Aussie teacher at school.

CORNELIA. Oh.

LAURA. Surprisingly charming.

PHILLIP. He told us all about dreamtime.

CORNELIA. And did it fascinate you?

PHILLIP. Yeah. I'm kind of interested in all that.

LAURA (*to* DENNIS). Has Marigold told you all about dreamtime?

ROGER. Who's Marigold?

LAURA. His new dental nurse from Darwin.

CORNELIA. We never got up that far.

LAURA. Very talented, apparently.

DENNIS. She is.

LAURA. And quite sweet.

DENNIS. You've hardly met her.

LAURA. Even though there is something of the marsupial about her.

PHILLIP. Big tits.

LAURA. Phillip!

ROGER. I could do with a filling.

CORNELIA. Do you know anything about dreamtime, Laura?

LAURA. No.

PHILLIP. Of course, there is a theory that time doesn't exist, not as we generally perceive it, anyhow. It's like each of our lives is already set up just waiting for us to step into. It's all out there, all decided for us. We kid ourselves we have a say in the matter, but in truth we don't have any choice at all.

ROGER. Bollocks! Course we do. Look, here's my finger, here's my nose, and I'm now choosing to stick it up there.

LAURA. Australia hasn't done you any favours, has it?

PHILLIP. But how do you know that wasn't already planned?

ROGER. Give us a break, Phil. This is education for you. Fills your head with bollocks.

LAURA. It obviously filled your head with bollocks, Roger, but some people know how to benefit from it.

ROGER. Forget about A-levels. Go out into the real world. Get a job. Much healthier.

LAURA. That is such an irresponsible thing to say.

ROGER. All this academic nonsense does your head in.

CORNELIA. I'm an academic now, so watch what you say.

DENNIS. Ignore him, Phil. He was a star pupil in spite of himself. He got the best grades of his year.

PHILLIP. You didn't go to university, though, did you?

DENNIS. That's because Daddy made him an offer he couldn't refuse.

ROGER. And I've never looked back since.

CORNELIA. What do you do, Frank?

FRANK. I'm a writer.

CORNELIA. A writer! What do you write?

FRANK. Plays.

CORNELIA. Plays! I say! Would I have seen any?

FRANK. No, I don't think so.

CORNELIA. You never know. Come on, try me.

LAURA. Phillip, what about your photos?

PHILLIP. Oh yeah.

CORNELIA. Go on, Frank. Throw a few titles at me.

LAURA. Then we really ought to go, alright, Dennis?

DENNIS. Alright.

CORNELIA. I love theatre. I wish Roger liked it more, (*To* ROGER.) but it just doesn't do anything for you, does it, popsy?

ROGER. I prefer the pub.

CORNELIA. Do you like theatre, Phillip?

LAURA. He's a very good actor, actually.

PHILLIP. Mum!

LAURA. He played Mercutio in 'Romeo and Juliet.' He was fantastic.

PHILLIP. Mum!

DENNIS. You were good, Phil.

LAURA. I was so proud of you. I thought, 'My God, I've bred another Brad Pitt!'

CORNELIA. Ooh, I'd like to breed a Brad Pitt.

ROGER. I'd like you to breed a Pamela Anderson.

CORNELIA. Honestly! Now, Frank –

LAURA. Phillip, your photos.

CORNELIA. I wish you'd tell me. It's not every day I meet a playwright.

FRANK. Well, the last thing I wrote – a few years ago now – was something called 'A Piece of Cake.'

CORNELIA. Where was it on?

FRANK. The Palladian.

CORNELIA. The Palladium! Did you hear that, Roger?

FRANK. The Palladian. It's a pub. In Enfield.

CORNELIA. Oh.

ROGER. Sounds like my kind of theatre.

CORNELIA. 'A Piece of Cake.' What was it about?

FRANK. Proust, basically. A fictitious meeting between Proust and – and myself, actually.

LAURA. It was very good, wasn't it, Dennis?

DENNIS. Yes.

ROGER. Fucking Proust.

CORNELIA. Roger!

ROGER. Boring as batshit. Sorry, Frank, but –

FRANK. He's not everyone's cup of tea.

ROGER. You're not kidding. We did him in French. Someone should have shoved that madeleine right up his fucking arse.

LAURA. Roger, will you please watch your language?

CORNELIA. He's always like this on red wine.

ROGER. One of his sentences was so long, I'd grown half an inch by the time I reached the end of it.

LAURA. Phillip, if you don't show us your photos now –

ROGER. Talk about ego! Jesus Christ! Always writing about himself. I mean, who gives a toss if a whiff of his Aunt Léonie's old knickers sent him off into a four-volume reverie?

LAURA. You've made your point.

ROGER. Pampered, bedridden Mummy's boy! I'd have given him a smack in the mouth. Fucked up little snob!

DENNIS. Roger –

ROGER. Mind you, if you think about it, we're all fucked up, aren't we?

CORNELIA. Roger!

ROGER. Give us a drink, Den.

LAURA. Honestly!

DENNIS *obliges.*

ROGER. You see, the problem is, we've got nothing to fight for anymore.

LAURA. Oh my God . . .

ROGER. That's the problem. I mean, look at us: classless snobs. (*Re.* DENNIS.) The Dentist. (*Re.* CORNELIA.) The Designer. (*Re.* FRANK.) The Writer. (*Re. himself.*) The Wine Dealer. (*Re.* LAURA.) The . . . Anyway, we're floating around, not knowing our arses from our elbows, cos we've turned our backs on our real selves and now don't know who the fuck we are. Still, what's it matter? I tell you, Phil, the only thing you need to learn is that, when it comes down to it, you're on your own, and if you understand that, you'll be alright. Do you know, Laura, you're looking sexy as fuck?

He has a glug of wine, then a mouthful of crisps. Pause.

CORNELIA. Have you read 'Beowulf'?

FRANK. No.

CORNELIA.
> 'Ðaem eafera wæs æfter cenned
> geong in geardum, þone God sende
> folce tō frōfre.'

Isn't that wonderful? I studied it at night school in Sydney on my Anglo-Saxon course. It's fascinating. If you ever get the chance.

FRANK. Yes.

CORNELIA. I'm going to carry on up in Edinburgh. I don't want to let it go. Have you been to night school, Laura?

LAURA. I don't have the time.

CORNELIA. Have you, Dennis?

DENNIS. No.

CORNELIA. Have you, Frank?

FRANK. . . . Yes.

CORNELIA. Oh! What did you do?

FRANK. Playwrighting Skills.

CORNELIA. Oh.

FRANK. I still go, as it happens.

LAURA. Phillip, photos.

CORNELIA. It must be quite hard to make a living as a writer.

FRANK. Yes, it is. I do some teaching to make –

CORNELIA. Oh! What do you teach?

FRANK. English.

CORNELIA. Oh!

FRANK. To foreign students.

CORNELIA. Oh.

LAURA. Phillip!

PHILLIP. Yeah. Right.

He sorts through his photos.

CORNELIA. I love photos.

FRANK. Have you been to Madrid?

CORNELIA. No, I don't like bullfighting.

DENNIS. That shouldn't stop you going.

CORNELIA. I just don't like the idea of being near it. The thought that I might be looking at a Velasquez or having a paella a few streets away from a bull being murdered . . . (*Shuddering.*) Ooh . . .

FRANK. Murdered?

LAURA. You've just spent several years in a country where they kill kangaroos.

CORNELIA. Yes, but they don't put on tight trousers and do it in rings.

PHILLIP. It's fantastic.

LAURA. What is?

PHILLIP. Bullfighting.

CORNELIA. Phillip, you didn't go to a bullfight, did you?

PHILLIP. Yeah. It's incredible.

CORNELIA (*upset*). Oh . . .

LAURA. You didn't mention it.

PHILLIP. It was just part of the holiday. We did loads of things.

LAURA. You went just the once?

PHILLIP. Once or twice.

CORNELIA (*more upset*). Oh . . .

PHILLIP. Sanchez's family are aficionados. They taught me all about it.

LAURA. But Sanchez is such a mousey little thing. I wouldn't have thought it'd be his bag at all.

PHILLIP. He's a big fan. Took me through it step by step. It's amazing.

CORNELIA. Those poor bulls . . .

PHILLIP. It gets you right in the gut, like nothing I've ever seen.

ROGER. That's right.

CORNELIA. How do you know?

ROGER *shrugs.*

You haven't been to one, have you?

ROGER. Just the once.

CORNELIA. When?

ROGER. On a school trip to Spain.

DENNIS. Oh, I remember you going on that trip. You bought Mum a fan –

CORNELIA. The school took you to a bullfight?

ROGER. No.

DENNIS. And Dad a chorizo.

ROGER. A few of us snuck off to see what it was all about.

DENNIS. And me bugger all, I seem to remember.

CORNELIA. Oh, Roger!

ROGER. I didn't kill the bull myself.

LAURA. Let's see the photos.

CORNELIA. Not if they're of bullfighting, thank you very much!

PHILLIP *hands* LAURA *a photo.*

PHILLIP. That's Sanchez outside – somewhere or other.

LAURA (*passing it on, as she does with each one*). You see, he is mousey.

PHILLIP. And this is Sanchez outside . . . Anyway, it's Sanchez.

LAURA. Are there any of you?

PHILLIP. Yeah. This is Sanchez, and there's me, and we're in that big square thing.

LAURA. What big square thing?

PHILLIP. A sort of square, y'know.

DENNIS. Plaza Mayor.

PHILLIP. Yeah. No, another one.

LAURA. Who took it?

PHILLIP. His sister.

LAURA. I thought she was away.

PHILLIP. Yeah. She's studying in Buenos Aires, but she was home for the summer. That's me in a market.

LAURA. Did Sanchez take that?

PHILLIP. Er . . . yeah –

LAURA. No, he couldn't have. He's there in the background looking at the puppies.

CORNELIA. Puppies! Let me see.

LAURA *passes her the photo.*

LAURA. So who did take it?

PHILLIP. Dunno. And this is –

CORNELIA. Oh, no!

ROGER. What's wrong?

CORNELIA. The puppies! They're all in cages, squashed together like sardines. Poor little things! What do they do to them?

PHILLIP. Eat them.

CORNELIA (*appalled*). Oh!

DENNIS. Phillip!

PHILLIP. They sell them. They sell birds and monkeys too. It's unbelievable, this market.

CORNELIA. Monkeys!

PHILLIP. This is me having a coffee.

LAURA. Where's Sanchez?

PHILLIP. . . . He stayed in that day, that's right.

LAURA. Stayed in?

PHILLIP. Yeah. Got the runs.

LAURA. So who took it?

PHILLIP. His sister.

LAURA. What's that?

PHILLIP. Where?

LAURA. On the table.

PHILLIP. 'T's a cup of coffee.

LAURA. In the ashtray.

PHILLIP. Oh. That's a cigarette.

LAURA. Your cigarette?

PHILLIP. No. His sister's. And this is –

 LAURA *takes it from him.*

 . . . at a pool. It's me.

LAURA. Yes, I can see that.

PHILLIP. Sunbathing.

LAURA. Who took it?

PHILLIP. His sister. (*Re. the next photo.*) And this one's –

LAURA (*still on the pool photo*). I suppose that packet of cigarettes is hers too.

PHILLIP. Yeah, it is.

ROGER. Bet you're glad you got these out, eh, Phil?

CORNELIA. Do you smoke, Frank?

FRANK. I used to.

PHILLIP (*re. next photo*). Anyway, this is –

CORNELIA. Do you, Dennis?

DENNIS. No.

CORNELIA. Do you, Laura?

LAURA (*studying the pool photo intently*). What?

CORNELIA. Smoke.

LAURA. No.

CORNELIA. Well, that's the thing, you see: either you do or you don't.

LAURA (*re. the pool photo*). What is that?

PHILLIP. What?

LAURA (*pointing*). That.

PHILLIP. A smudge.

LAURA. It doesn't look like a smudge to me.

ROGER. Let's have a look.

LAURA (*not letting him*). What is it?

PHILLIP. Dunno.

LAURA. Phillip.

PHILLIP. What?

LAURA. There's something at the top of your leg on the inside of your thigh and I want to know what it is.

PHILLIP. 'T's a birthmark.

LAURA. Phillip!

DENNIS *takes it off her.*

What is it?

Beat.

PHILLIP (*muttering*). Tattoo.

LAURA. Excuse me?

PHILLIP. It's a tattoo.

LAURA. A tattoo?

> PHILLIP *nods.*

> What does it say?

PHILLIP. Adelaida.

LAURA. And who is Adelaida?

> *Pause.*

PHILLIP. His sister.

LAURA. Jesus Christ!

ROGER. Let's see.

> DENNIS *gives it to him.*

PHILLIP. It's only a couple of centimetres.

LAURA. The length is not the point.

ROGER. Some people think so.

LAURA. How could you think of doing such a thing, disfiguring yourself like that?

DENNIS. Come on –

LAURA. What do you mean, 'Come on'?

PHILLIP. It's only a tattoo.

ROGER. I've got one.

LAURA. What's that got to do with it?

ROGER. I had it done in Sydney.

CORNELIA. Isn't that a coincidence?

ROGER. A little koala.

CORNELIA. On his bottom.

ROGER (*indicating*). Just there.

CORNELIA. So sweet. He's chewing a eucalyptus leaf.

FRANK. Did it hurt?

ROGER (*enthusiastically*). Yeah!

CORNELIA. We call him Colin.

LAURA. Will you shut up for a minute!

DENNIS. Laura.

LAURA. I'm going to phone Sanchez's father.

PHILLIP. No, Mum.

LAURA. This is an absolute outrage. How could he allow it to happen?

PHILLIP. He didn't know anything about it. It was all my idea. It was a joke. It's got nothing to do with Señor Morales.

LAURA. His daughter's a grown woman!

PHILLIP. She's only twenty-two.

LAURA. And she's given free rein to mess about with my son.

PHILLIP. It wasn't like that.

LAURA (*to* DENNIS). Haven't you got anything to say?

DENNIS. Well –

LAURA. I can't believe this is happening.

PHILLIP. We didn't do anything. She just – joined in from time to time.

LAURA. So why is her name emblazoned across your crotch?

PHILLIP. It was a joke. That's all.

LAURA. I am so disappointed in you.

She walks out. We hear her going upstairs and slamming a door.

PHILLIP. Anyway, it'll come off – won't it?

ROGER. Yeah. They do it with lasers.

PHILLIP. It's only a fucking tattoo.

He walks out. We hear him stamping upstairs and slamming a door. Pause.

ROGER. Want to see the bike?

DENNIS *nods and follows* ROGER *out.*

CORNELIA. Do you live around here, Frank?

FRANK. No. The other side of town.

CORNELIA. Oh. Whereabouts?

FRANK. Snaresbrook.

CORNELIA (*pityingly*). Ah.

Beat.

Do you have a partner?

FRANK. No.

CORNELIA (*again pityingly*). Don't you?

FRANK. It's not a problem.

CORNELIA. That's good.

Beat.

Is Frank short for anything?

FRANK. No.

CORNELIA. It's nice being called by your full name, isn't it?

FRANK. I've never thought about it.

CORNELIA. Lots of people call Roger Rog, but I don't. His name's Roger and that's what I call him. And our child, whatever he or she might be called, will be what he or she is called. Australians tend to shorten everything, you know.

FRANK. Do they?

CORNELIA. Yes. Breakfast's brekky, chicken's chook, this afternoon's this arvo, and Roger was always Rog. I was Corny.

FRANK. Really.

CORNELIA. And sometimes Cor. Silly, isn't it? And then there are some words that they make longer, but I can't remember what they are.

The sound of the bike being revved.

People think I'm stupid, you know.

FRANK. Do they?

CORNELIA. Because I'm female and I've got a funny voice, but it doesn't bother me because I know I'm not.

FRANK. Obviously you're not.

CORNELIA. And if they got to know me, they'd realize it. Who's to say what an interior designer, fluent in Anglo-Saxon, should sound like?

FRANK. You're probably more intelligent than the whole lot of us.

She helps herself to a mouthful from one of the bowls and instantly spits it out.

That's pot pourri.

CORNELIA. Ugh!

She rinses her mouth with her drink.

FRANK. Are you alright?

CORNELIA. Yes, yes.

FRANK. Would you like some water?

CORNELIA. No, I'm fine, thank you. They look just like those funny crisps, don't they?

More revving from outside.

Roger understands me. That's why I love him so much. I can't tell you, Frank, how happy I am that we're having a baby. You can't imagine the joy of having a part of Roger inside me.

More revving.

Anyway . . .

Beat.

I've worked hard to get where I am. I expect you have too.

FRANK. Yes, except that I haven't really got anywhere. Not for want of trying.

Revving.

CORNELIA. He does love his bikes.

FRANK. Of course there are some people who don't seem to have to work at anything. Phillip, for example. He picks things up just like that, whereas I've always had to graft.

CORNELIA. Yes.

FRANK. I sometimes wonder why I bother. It takes years to get an idea, years to write the bloody thing, then you're lucky if it gets read, and then they'll say, 'It's not quite for us, but we'd be interested in reading your next one,' and you think, 'But it nearly killed me writing this one.' Of course it's not always like that; you might hit the jackpot and get twenty performances in some clapped out dive in the suburbs. Still, no one's holding a gun to my head.

Beat.

I saved his life, you know.

CORNELIA. Phillip?

FRANK. Yes.

CORNELIA. No, I didn't know.

FRANK. We were swimming in the reservoir, a few months ago now, and suddenly he disappeared. I dived under and dragged him out and – well, gave him the kiss of life.

CORNELIA. That's amazing. Have you learnt First Aid?

FRANK. No, no. I just – put my mouth over his – instinctively. Anyone would've, I think.

CORNELIA. Well . . .

Beat.

Have you thought of trying contact ads?

LAURA *enters. She clocks the two of them.*

You know, Laura, I was thinking, if you put a door in that wall there, and another one in the next room, you'd have a bit of an enfilade. That'd be nice, wouldn't it? Anyway . . .

She goes out.

LAURA. Imagine living with that!

FRANK. She's alright.

LAURA. Enfilade, my arse! Oh Frank, how could he do that to himself?

FRANK. He's young.

LAURA. We're all young at some stage, but we don't go around branding ourselves.

FRANK. He's impetuous, headstrong. It's the sort of thing he'd do.

LAURA. It's the sort of thing Roger would do, but Phillip! It's so stupid. That beautiful skin!

FRANK. And it's not that visible. You'd have to look to find it. I mean, not everyone's going to see it, are they? Admittedly some people will, but then – well –

LAURA. I knew he couldn't have been to the Prado that many times. Every phone call was, 'Oh, we went to the Prado again.' He was lying to me, Frank. And I bet he hardly saw poor little Sanchez. He and Adelaida probably sent him off with some nachos and a handful of pesetas while they got up to all sorts in the Ramblas – when they weren't watching bulls being slaughtered.

FRANK. Aren't nachos Mexican?

LAURA. Oh, whatever.

FRANK. And the Ramblas are in Barcelona.

LAURA. I don't care if they're in fucking Brixton! The point is that this Spanish harpy has seduced my son and left her trademark on his testicles.

FRANK. Not quite.

LAURA. Give or take an inch. The thought of some greasy old man pricking my son's thigh with needles, and that harlot leering in the background with a fag in her mouth – oh God! Needles! What if they were infected?

FRANK. For God's sake!

LAURA. I'm sorry, Frank, but needles in a backstreet in Madrid!

FRANK. Why should it be more dangerous in Madrid? Millions of people get tattooed and they don't catch anything. Look at Roger; he's alright.

LAURA. That's a matter of opinion. I feel so betrayed. How could he do this to me? He's the only person I can rely on, apart from you, and now look what he's gone and done!

FRANK. Laura, he's had a tattoo. He hasn't eaten a baby. Anyway, I think you can get rid of them now with lasers.

LAURA. They're inedible.

FRANK. Indelible.

LAURA. Indelible, whatever! We really must get to the restaurant.

FRANK. Don't let it spoil this evening. Listen, don't let it spoil anything. In the scheme of things, Laura, it's not important.

Beat.

LAURA. I suppose not. It's just so hard, letting go. And the awful thing is, this is just the beginning.

PHILLIP *has entered. He's holding a CD. She clocks him and turns away.* FRANK *suddenly feels out of place. Pause.*

PHILLIP. She taught me to tango as well.

LAURA. Oh my God!

PHILLIP. Mum, she's just a girl. She's nice. Honestly.

*Beat. He puts the CD on the hi fi: a tango. He slowly walks
over to* LAURA. *He tentatively touches her hand. She
snatches it away. Beat. He tries again. This time she allows
him to touch her. He gently pulls her round to face him. He
puts an arm around her waist and very slowly moves to the
music. She impassively follows his lead. He gradually gains
confidence and guides her through a few steps. She picks
them up with relative ease.* FRANK *looks on. Soon they're
dancing quite well together, eye to eye. At one point*
LAURA *suddenly takes the lead and executes a fairly
extreme manoeuvre with him.*

Blimey, where d'you learn that?

LAURA. Oh, I've tangoed in my time.

They laugh and proceed to throw themselves into it.
DENNIS *appears. He takes in the scene and, unnoticed,
exits into the kitchen.* FRANK *watches them as they dance,
their eyes still fixed on each other, and the lights fade. The
music continues as the lights come up on:*

The Kitchen

DENNIS *is sitting at the kitchen table, dead still, expression-
less. The tango can be heard from the sitting-room.* FRANK
*enters and is surprised to see him. They silently acknowledge
each other.* FRANK *is unsure whether to stay.*

DENNIS. So how are you?

FRANK. Oh. I'm well, thanks.

Beat.

DENNIS. It's going okay then?

FRANK. Fine.

DENNIS. Good. That's good.

Beat.

No side effects or . . . ?

FRANK. No. Not yet, anyway.

Beat.

It's a bit of a leap in the dark, of course. For everyone, really, doctors included. I suppose I could wake up one morning with no teeth or a hump on my back or an extra eye or something. But so far, so good.

DENNIS. Yes.

FRANK. Yes.

DENNIS. Do you know Primrose Hill?

FRANK. . . . I've been there – once or twice, but – no, not really.

DENNIS. I . . .

DENNIS puts his hand to his mouth.

FRANK. Are you alright?

DENNIS nods. Beat. He takes his hand away.

DENNIS. Sorry.

FRANK. There's no –

DENNIS. Sorry.

FRANK. – no problem.

DENNIS gets up and shuts the door. Beat.

DENNIS. Madrid's a marvellous city.

FRANK. Yes.

DENNIS. Marvellous.

FRANK. Yes. Yes, I've heard it's marvellous.

DENNIS. Yes.

Beat.

I haven't been since Franco, if truth were told, but I would imagine it's – it's still marvellous.

FRANK. Yes, I'm sure it is.

DENNIS. Yes.

Beat.

You know, he'd never sleep – never sleep without her at his side. One couldn't blame him, of course. She's always doted on him and always will, no doubt. But if she wasn't there, he'd scream and scream for his Mummy. I'd never have believed how lonely one could feel. It won't be too long before he's calling me 'the old man'.

FRANK. I'm sure he – he thinks as much of you as he does of Laura. I'm sure he does. It must be wonderful to have a son like him.

Beat.

DENNIS. It's a funny business.

Beat.

FRANK. Dennis, why did you mention Primrose Hill?

DENNIS. Mm. I think I'm losing her. Yes. I'm losing her.

Pause.

One day, very shortly after we'd first met, in fact – that time I did some root-canal work for her . . . This particular day, an afternoon, we were sitting on top of Primrose Hill – it was the height of summer – and saw the most extraordinary thing: at the foot of the hill was a layer of snow, a vast expanse of thick white snow glistening in the sunlight. The middle of summer, it was, a hot July afternoon, and we were amazed. And I looked at her and thought, this is the most remarkable woman and I love her more than – more than . . . well . . . The snow – so strange. I thought we were blessed. I'm looking forward to my cous-cous.

FRANK. What was it? A freak snowstorm or – ?

DENNIS. A trick of the light. That's all it was. I'm having a relationship.

FRANK. Are you?

DENNIS. With Marigold.

FRANK. Oh.

DENNIS. She's a marvellous girl. Only nineteen. The best nurse I've had. She looks nothing like a marsupial. You won't tell Laura, will you?

FRANK. No, I won't tell her.

DENNIS. Thanks. So I'll be leaving her.

FRANK. Laura?

DENNIS. Yes. I love her to death, you know. One day she'll come round to loving me.

PHILLIP enters.

PHILLIP. Mum said we ought to go.

DENNIS. Yes, we should. Right.

He leaves. PHILLIP *takes a handful of crisps from an open bag on the kitchen table and stuffs them in his mouth. He goes to the fridge and takes out a bottle of beer.* FRANK *looks on.* PHILLIP *knocks off the bottle-top on the edge of the table. The froth oozes out. He swigs it. As he turns to* FRANK, *he suddenly finds himself in a clinch,* FRANK *kissing him passionately. He feverishly explores* PHILLIP's *body, then rubs his crotch. The kiss continues as they stagger back against the table, shifting it slightly. After a long time,* FRANK *takes his mouth from* PHILLIP's *and steps back.*

FRANK. Thanks for the postcard.

PHILLIP. 'T's okay.

He swigs his beer.

FRANK. It looked nice, the railway station.

PHILLIP. I couldn't remember the one you asked for.

FRANK. Antonello de Messina's 'The Dead Christ Held by an Angel.'

PHILLIP. Oh, yeah.

FRANK. But it doesn't matter. It was nice you sent me one at all – what with everything that was going on.

PHILLIP. How are you?

FRANK. I'm fine.

PHILLIP. Drugs alright?

FRANK. Yes. So far.

He touches the wooden table-top. PHILLIP *flinches.*

I'm touching wood.

PHILLIP. Sorry. Better get ready.

FRANK. So will you be keeping in touch?

PHILLIP. Who with?

FRANK. Adelaida.

PHILLIP. Dunno.

FRANK. You will, won't you?

PHILLIP. Dunno. Maybe. You shouldn't have done that.

FRANK. You didn't seem to mind.

PHILLIP. You shouldn't have done it.

FRANK. You were getting a hard-on.

PHILLIP. I'm always getting a hard-on; I'm fifteen.

FRANK. Nearly sixteen.

PHILLIP. We've got to go.

FRANK. I've started dreaming about you.

PHILLIP. Jesus! I thought we said we'd forget about it.

FRANK. I'm afraid it's not that easy.

PHILLIP. I told you, it didn't mean anything. It doesn't mean anything.

FRANK. Well, that's gratitude for you.

PHILLIP. What are you talking about?

FRANK. You'd be dead if it weren't for me.

PHILLIP. No, I bloody wouldn't! I was fine and you know it, but you didn't give me a chance. You were attached to my face before I could say a word, like something out of *Alien*.

FRANK. You'd nearly drowned.

PHILLIP. I was winded, that's all.

FRANK. I saved your life. You know I did. You needed resuscitating.

PHILLIP. Since when did resuscitation involve a tongue down the throat?

FRANK. You're the one who started it with the tongues.

PHILLIP. Bollocks!

FRANK. You did.

PHILLIP. You'd got me pissed.

FRANK. Come off it!

PHILLIP. We've got to go.

They don't move.

Things have changed. It's different. I was younger then.

FRANK. It was two months ago!

PHILLIP. Yeah, but I feel older now cos of – y'know . . .

FRANK. Adelaida.

PHILLIP. Look, Frank, you're very nice. I really like you – I really, really like you – and I'm really grateful you helped me get through my French GCSE, but what happened at the reservoir – it was nothing. It was a mistake.

FRANK. You enjoyed it.

PHILLIP. There was nothing to enjoy. Nothing happened.

FRANK. You were all over me like a cheap suit.

PHILLIP. I'm at that sort of age. I'd shag a rat given half the chance.

FRANK. Thanks a lot.

PHILLIP. It's over, forgotten, okay?

FRANK. Life's not like that.

PHILLIP. We've got to go.

He turns to go. FRANK *stops him.*

FRANK. Phillip, just once – let's meet up – just one more time –

PHILLIP. For fuck's sake –

FRANK. Please –

PHILLIP. No.

FRANK. Just one more time. Please.

PHILLIP. No!

FRANK. Then let me see your tattoo.

PHILLIP. Frank –

FRANK. Go on.

PHILLIP. Stop it, please.

FRANK. Let me see it –

PHILLIP. We've got to go.

FRANK. – and that'll be it, I promise.

Once again PHILLIP *starts to go and* FRANK *tries to stop him.*

PHILLIP (*roughly shaking him off*). No!

As PHILLIP's *about to walk out:*

FRANK. I'm not well, for fuck's sake!

PHILLIP *stops.*

PHILLIP. You said you were.

FRANK. Yes, but for how long? It isn't a cure, you know. I could build up a resistance and start getting infected all over again and then where would I be? There are only a limited amount of options left. The truth of the matter is, I'm probably not going to be around for that long. I have to make the most of everything. You do understand that, don't you, Phillip? You do, don't you?

PHILLIP (*muttering*). Yeah.

FRANK. I know I probably seem as if I'm coping, as if it's all okay, but believe me, I need support, I need comfort – I really do. At the reservoir, I know you were a bit drunk, and I know we probably shouldn't have, but it was alright, wasn't it?

Beat.

Wasn't it?

PHILLIP *shrugs.*

We're friends, that's all – I'm not suggesting we should be anything else – and I have been a good friend to you, I hope. Haven't I?

PHILLIP. Yeah.

FRANK. I've always tried to be there for you, like when things haven't been great with your Mum and Dad, and . . . well, you know.

Beat.

I only want to see your tattoo. That's not too much to ask, is it? Please.

PHILLIP. Someone might come in.

FRANK (*indicating the pantry*). We can go in there.

Beat.

PHILLIP. Just for a second, right?

FRANK. Right.

Businesslike, PHILLIP *goes into the pantry followed by* FRANK, *who shuts the door behind them.* PHILLIP *drops his trousers.*

PHILLIP. There you go.

> FRANK *kneels to inspect it.*

FRANK. It's quite neat, isn't it?

PHILLIP. Okay?

FRANK. Let me just . . .

> *He gently touches it.*

> She's a lucky girl.

PHILLIP. We'd better –

> FRANK *licks it.* LAURA *comes into the kitchen.*

LAURA. Phillip! Darling!

> FRANK *and* PHILLIP *freeze.*

> Where the hell . . . ? (*Going out.*) Phillip!

PHILLIP (*hurriedly pulling up and fastening his trousers*). That's it. Alright? Got that?

> PHILLIP *rushes out of the pantry, across the kitchen, and disappears into the garden.*

FRANK (*rising panic*). Oh my God! What the fuck am I . . . ? Jesus . . . Jesus –

LAURA (*off*). Phillip!

> FRANK *comes out of the pantry shutting the door behind him.* LAURA *pops her head round the door.*

> Do you know where Phillip is?

FRANK. No, I don't.

LAURA (*walking in*). We'll lose our table. Are you alright?

FRANK. Yes.

LAURA. What about the tango, eh?

FRANK. It was very good.

LAURA. You've got a bit of crisp on your mouth.(*Wiping it off.*) Mucky boy.

FRANK. Thanks.

LAURA. He's going to break a few hearts.

FRANK. Yes.

LAURA. The little devil! (*Calling.*) Phillip!

As she walks out, she does a little shimmy.

Phillip!

Fade. Lights up on:

The Restaurant

FRANK *and* GOMPERTZ *at the moment we left them.*
FRANK *has the dressing over his left eye;* GOMPERTZ *is
on his mobile.*

GOMPERTZ. . . . Great . . . Ciao.

He puts his mobile away.

Thank God for that!

FRANK. Everything alright?

GOMPERTZ. I mislaid a little something, but the night sister's
found it, bless her. The thought of a whole ward whizzed
off its face! Sorry, you were saying . . .

FRANK. Where was I?

GOMPERTZ (*taking the inhaler from* FRANK). A dreadful do,
or something or other.

FRANK. Yes. My friend Laura – this do she had . . . Have you
ever done anything you were ashamed of?

GOMPERTZ. Oh yes. Yes. Just about everything.

He takes a snort from the inhaler.

FRANK. What you said – the blink of an eyelid and life's
changed forever –

GOMPERTZ. There always seems to be that little surprise round the corner: the unrevealed secret –

FRANK. Yes.

GOMPERTZ. A double-decker bus –

FRANK. You see, at this do –

GOMPERTZ. We never seem to get beyond this point, do we?

FRANK. What happened – was just awful – unimaginably tragic. It's haunted me for a year. And the point is – I think it'd make quite a good play. You see, I'm coming round to the opinion that I have to use whatever's thrown at me.

GOMPERTZ *hands him the inhaler.*

Thank you.

He snorts.

GOMPERTZ. I might plump for the Corned Beef Hash.

FRANK. I'm right, aren't I?

GOMPERTZ. No, you're not. You're making a terrible mistake.

FRANK. I'm not talking about the medication.

GOMPERTZ. Look at the arse on that!

FRANK. It's no good, I've got to tell her. I've got to come clean about it. Tomorrow I'm going to go over there and I'm going to tell her.

GOMPERTZ. You still haven't told me what it was.

FRANK. No. Well, this do – a year ago –

His pager bleeps.

GOMPERTZ. Jesus Christ!

He checks it.

Sorry.

He dials a number on his mobile.

FRANK. It doesn't matter.

GOMPERTZ (*into his mobile*). Yeah? . . . Yes . . .

FRANK. Anyway . . .

GOMPERTZ (*into his mobile*). Fuck it! The silly queen hasn't
been taking his septrin . . . (*Looking at his watch.*) Alright,
I'll be there in –

*Blackout as the sound of a motorbike cuts in, very loud. It
starts fading into the distance as the lights come up on:*

The Kitchen

LAURA *and* FRANK *at the moment we left them at the end
of the first scene, he with his eye bandage, she removing her
sunglasses. They listen as the bike fades into silence. Pause.
The piano starts up again from another part of the house: the
faltering rendition of the Aria from Bach's Goldberg Variations.
We become aware, as before, of the sounds of summer gardens:
the sprinkler system, a strimmer, children playing and
birdsong.*

LAURA. Phphillip . . . Phphillip . . . (*She has a stammer.*)
Exxactly a year ago . . . Phph . . . Phph . . .

FRANK *looks helplessly on.*

Every dday – mminute – I wonder if he mmeant to – or if
he wwas doing it jjust for the ththrill . . . or if ssomething
had upsset him and he'd chch-chchosen to – to . . . or was it
an accident wwaiting to happen? And I wwonder if, just ffor
a moment, as he was ssspeeding along, I may have ccrossed
his mind. I hope it was for the ththrill of it. The ththought of
him being in ddespair . . . I wanted him to knnow that life
ccould be happy, but that sseems to be – the hardest lesson
to learn.

Beat.

FRANK. He was happy. I'm sure he was.

A drawer ejects itself from the kitchen-table and smashes on the floor, scattering cutlery and making them jump out of their skin. The piano stops. They stare at the mess, then:

LAURA. (*shouting*). It's alright. Everyththing's alright.

Beat. The piano starts again.

FRANK. Shall I . . . ?

LAURA. Don't worry. I can ddo it. Honestly. I know you have to ggo.

FRANK. Laura.

LAURA. Yes?

FRANK. There's something I want to tell you –

ROGER *appears from the garden, taking them by surprise.*

ROGER. Morning.

FRANK. Roger.

ROGER. Hello, Marcel. (*Re. the bandage.*) Slipped with the eyeliner? Hello, Laura.

FRANK *suddenly winces and holds his stomach.*

FRANK. Sorry. Just need to . . .

ROGER. Touch of the tomtits?

He's gone. Beat. LAURA *starts to pick up the cutlery.* ROGER *watches her.*

LAURA. Wwhat brings you here?

ROGER. I was in town for a meeting, so I thought I'd pop in and say hello, so – hello.(*Re. the piano playing.*) Still got Liberace in the attic, then?

Beat.

I'll give you a hand.

He starts to help her.

LAURA. There's no need.

ROGER. I know.

Beat.

LAURA. How's Ccornelia?

ROGER. She's fine. Sends her love. She's – fine.

They continue in silence, then he stops and looks at her.

LAURA. Wwould you like a – ?

ROGER. No. (*Re. the ejected drawer.*) This, I presume –

LAURA. It's nothing. But the ssooner we leave this house, ththe better.

She stops too. Beat.

ROGER. Cornelia – she's changed, you know, since the miscarriage. Quite a bit. It's like she's gone into herself. She's not interested in work anymore.

LAURA. That might be a phphase.

ROGER. Yeah. It might be. I try and do things to please her, but I don't always get it right. It's a drag sometimes, I tell you. I went with her to a piano recital a few weeks ago. The whole evening was devoted to a piece that was supposed to be an exact imitation of birdsong. It sounded nothing like bloody birds – well, no birds I've ever heard. Two fucking hours of plinkety-plonk, the sort of sound Cornelia makes when she's dusting the keyboard. It nearly drove me mad. I was twitching by the end.

LAURA. Ccome on –

ROGER. It's true. I didn't stop till I went to bed. That's another thing, of course: she won't let me touch her any more.

LAURA. She nneeds time.

ROGER. Yeah. It's been months though.

LAURA. Then she needs mmore time.

ROGER. Yeah.

Beat. He looks at her, then turns away.

She's got a cat. Nice little thing. Sort of – furry. She calls it Smudge.

Beat.

Takes it everywhere.

LAURA. Not to the rrecital, I hope. Mmight have scared the birds.

They smile briefly. Unsure what to say, they look out at the garden. FRANK's appeared, unnoticed, in the kitchen doorway. He watches them.

ROGER. I'd loved to have sat with my son, and have him tell me this and that, how much his mother pissed him off, or how he'd fallen for some girl and she was driving him mad and what should he do, and I'd have told him I was the last bloody person to ask . . . Still, it's not to be.

FRANK *slips into the pantry to hide and listen.*

If only I hadn't have left those fucking keys lying around!

Beat.

I'm sorry.

LAURA. No.

ROGER. I'm sorry.

Beat.

LAURA. On days like this he'd llie for hours, a hand across his eyes, ffloating away.

ROGER. You know, since we met, a day hasn't passed when I haven't thought about you.

LAURA (*nervously checking they're alone*). Pplease –

ROGER. It's true.

LAURA. I don't wwant to hear –

ROGER. I promise you.

LAURA. No –

ROGER. That day we made love –

LAURA (*putting her finger to his mouth*). Sh –

ROGER. Seventeen years ago –

LAURA. Roger, pplease –

ROGER. It was seventeen years ago.

LAURA. Yyyes.

ROGER. That's right.

LAURA. Ssseventeen.

ROGER. Yes.

> *Beat.* FRANK *is riveted.*

> I have spent years of my life with a woman who isn't even my type. And so little time with my boy.

> *Beat.*

> I'm right, aren't I?

> *For a moment, the piano seems to get louder. She looks at him, is about to speak, then subsides against him. The piano and the other sounds fade as, from far in the distance, we hear the tango. Very gently they start to sway,* LAURA *hanging limply in his arms.* FRANK *tentatively peers out of the pantry to see what's happening. The tango fades and they're still. In silence they look into each other's eyes.* FRANK *doesn't move a muscle. Suddenly the piano strikes up with a few bars of the tango, crudely rendered, breaking their reverie. They part as* FRANK *darts out of sight.*

LAURA (*looking round*). Ffrank might –

ROGER. It's alright, 't's alright.

> *Beat.*

> I've got to go.

> *A moment as they look at each other.*

LAURA. I'm sure Ddennis would like to ss –

ROGER. Next time, maybe.

He leaves through the garden. LAURA *watches him go as* FRANK *steps out of the pantry. The Bach resumes on the piano.*

FRANK (*pretending he's just come into the kitchen*). That's better. Suddenly hits you. I've had some near-misses, I can tell you. Where's Roger?

LAURA. He had to ggo.

FRANK. I know the feeling. I haven't seen him since – well, since last year.

LAURA. He's in town for a mmeeting.

FRANK. Anyway, I suppose I ought to make a move.

LAURA. Wasn't there something you wwanted to tell me?

Beat.

FRANK. Yes, there was. I – I wanted to tell you . . .

Beat. He kisses her.

. . . that you're the best friend I've had.

She holds him tightly.

LAURA. Ththank you for coming. It means so much. I rreally hope ththings work out for you.

They part.

FRANK. I'll probably be back in no time.

He makes to go.

It's strange, you know: in the garden, when we were sitting here, I thought I saw, for a second –

LAURA. Yes – it was Rroger.

FRANK. I know.

LAURA. He always ccomes that way.

FRANK. Yes, but for a second, it was Phillip I thought I saw.

Pause.

LAURA. Then you were mmistaken.

Beat.

FRANK. Anyway, I must be off.

She closes the kitchen door. Beat.

LAURA. It was – just the once, and he was – just a kkid. One moment of – wwell . . . I thought, 'Oh, there'll be other ttimes like this,' and mmade myself fforget. But you know, there haven't been; ththat was it. And ttry as I might, I can't stop wondering what if, what if . . . And Phphillip – he nnever knew. It's like a ppunishment.

The piano's stopped.

FRANK. No, you mustn't think that. It's not. It was an accident, a dreadful accident, and you can't spend your life – you can't spend your life feeling guilty.

LAURA. I do ttry – to ccome to terms, to mmake my peace –

DENNIS (*from another part of the house*). Laura! . . . Laura! . . .

She opens the kitchen door.

LAURA (*calling*). Alright, Ddennis. It's alright.

She lights a cigarette and sits again at the French windows. The Bach resumes. She puts on her sunglasses. FRANK sits next to her.

FRANK. I'll write.

LAURA. Yes. Your pplay –

FRANK. No. To you, I mean.

She looks at him and smiles, then they gaze out at the garden. The sounds of the summer's day murmur on.

So I – I'd better be off.

We hear the final bars of the Aria as the lights fade to black.

End.

A Nick Hern Book

Mouth to Mouth first published in Great Britain in 2001
as a paperback original by Nick Hern Books,
14 Larden Road, London W3 7ST, in association with
the Royal Court Theatre, London

Mouth to Mouth copyright © 2001 by Kevin Elyot

Kevin Elyot has asserted his right to be identified as
author of this work

Typeset by Country Setting, Kingsdown, Kent CT14 8ES
Printed and bound in Great Britain by Biddles of Guildford

ISBN 1 85459 617 9

A CIP catalogue is available from the British Library

CAUTION All rights whatsoever in this play are strictly
reserved. Requests to reproduce the text in whole or in part
should be addressed to the publisher.

Amateur Performing Rights   Applications for performance,
including readings and excerpts, by amateurs should be
addressed to the Performing Rights Manager, Nick Hern Books,
14 Larden Road, London W3 7ST, *fax* +44(020)8746-2006,
e-mail info@nickhernbooks.demon.co.uk, except as follows:
Australia Dominie Drama, 8 Cross Street, Brookvale 2100,
fax (2) 9905 5209, *e-mail* dominie@dominie.com.au
New Zealand: Play Bureau, PO Box 420, New Plymouth,
fax (6)753 2150, *e-mail* play.bureau.nz@xtra.co.nz
United States of America and Canada: The Agency at the
address below

Professional Performing Rights Applications for performance
by professionals in any medium and in any language throughout
the world should be addressed to The Agency, 24 Pottery Lane,
Holland Park, London W11 4LZ, *fax* +44 (020) 7727 9037

No performance of any kind may be given unless a licence has
been obtained. Applications should be made before rehearsals
begin. Publication of this play does not necessarily indicate its
availability for amateur performance.